Beyond Here
There Be Dragons
Navigating the uncharted waters of grief

Thomas John Dennis

Grief River, LLC
Galena, Illinois

Grief River, LLC Galena, Illinois USA

ISBN: 978-1-7360182-0-0
Library of Congress Control Number: 2020921586

Printed in the USA

DEDICATION

In memory of my parents
James and Joan Dennis

CONTENTS

ACKNOWLEDGMENTS

I had no idea how much work goes into writing and then rewriting a book. I need to thank so many people for their invaluable feedback and support; their input made this a much better resource. I want to especially thank Jeffrey Hadloc, RN; Mike Dennis, LCSW; and Theresa Dennis, LCPC; for their personal and professional support. Ernest Luther did a great job taking my ideas and translating them into beautiful and interesting illustrations. Several colleagues need to be acknowledged for sharing their professional feedback, including Elsa Baehr, PhD; Jennifer Feinberg, LCSW; Allison Gilbert; Josh Magariel, LCSW; Elizabeth Siegel Cohen, LCSW; and Junko Yokota, PhD. I would also like to thank Andrew Rorabaugh; and Rae Jean V. Sielen; at Populore Publishing for their copyediting and advice. Without the help and support of each of these people, this book would not be in your hands today. Lastly, I want to acknowledge all the bereaved who have shared their stories with me and inspire me every day. Thank you all.

In pursuit of the divine pearl,
one would be well advised
to search for dragons.

TJ Melvin

INTRODUCTION

I'm a Midwesterner, and only an infrequent visitor to either coast. So, you might think I know little about salt water or the ways of seafarers, but I have more experience with these than you might think. I work in what might be imaginatively described as a tide pool called "bereavement." In between the ebb tide and the flow, there are brief interludes of calm when the bereaved can catch a breath and brace themselves before the tide turns and the waves of grief come rolling in again. In these calmer moments, I listen to their stories, offer consolation and encouragement, and together we look for ways to make sense of and cope with their loss.

Sometimes people ask me, "How are you able to do what you do, day after day? It must be so depressing." The truth is, I love my job. Helping people makes my life meaningful and gives it purpose. Instead of feeling depressed at the end of the day, I leave work feeling grateful for the reminder that life is sacred and fragile. My clients teach me valuable life lessons about love and relationships, about heartbreak and resilience, about tenacity and hope. I step away from these encounters feeling inspired, humbled, and changed.

I didn't start out with the intention of becoming a grief counselor, so it's interesting for me to examine the *whys* and *hows* of where we eventually end up, versus where we thought we'd go in life. Life is full of transitions—each turn, each

3

decision is critical, because every choice we make will determine a different outcome. Some transitions are meticulously and methodically planned, while others we'd prefer to have avoided, but life thrusts them upon us nonetheless.

As I look back, the story I'm about to tell began when I was still a young man, struggling with a different sort of life transition of my own. A wise and patient spiritual advisor listened to me drone on for months about just about anything other than the issue I needed to address. Finally, he challenged me, "What are you afraid of? What are you avoiding? What's inside that needs to be let out—a tiger, perhaps?" "Tiger," I countered, "that's no tiger; it's more like a dragon!" The intensity of my response startled us both. He encouraged me to stop running away from my "dragon," to turn and face it lovingly, and to consider what it was trying to tell me. Intuitively, I knew he was speaking a truth, but I wanted no part of it at the time.

About a year later, while on retreat, I finally sat down with a sketchbook and tried to draw a picture of the dragon dwelling within me. At first, all I could imagine were two menacing eyes glowing in the dark. Eventually, a head and body began to emerge. Once I was able to visualize that dragon, I discovered that it was not as fierce and frightening as I had first thought. Looking at my sketch, I realized that this dragon had always been my most intimate and loyal companion—a guardian willing to stand at its post until I was ready to unlock the door to the dark labyrinth that lay between me and the next phase of my life. Visualizing what was so frightening was an essential first step, but as I look back on that particular life transition, it probably took another three years to complete the full transition. I went back to school, and in the intervening years between young adulthood and midlife, I embarked on the second phase of my life journey. Today, I companion people who feel overwhelmed with one of the most challenging life transitions. On occasion, I am charged with the delicate task of introducing them to their dragons.

The dragons I'm talking about are, of course, metaphors—word pictures that give shape to concepts or emotions that are otherwise too difficult to identify or explain. Dragons symbolize everything that scares us. They are the stuff of legends, demonized by people who are risk-averse, and sung about in epic poems by those who mustered up the courage to face their dragons anyway. They are chaos and mystery. They are the embodiment of all the dangers—real and imagined—we might face as we embark on a new phase of life.

Mapmakers of old used to draw images of dragons, too. They drew them along the margins of maps as a warning to illustrate what lay in wait for anyone who dares to venture into unexplored territory. "Beyond here," they cautioned, "there be dragons." The implication was clear: You have reached the boundary of everything we know about; you are entering into uncharted waters. No one knows what lies beyond this point, but whatever it is, it will probably eat you! Early explorers had to be willing to face their dragons and chart a new course through the unknown to obtain their hoped-for goal of gold and glory. We too must be willing to make our way through the unknown in order to reach our goals.

When a loved one dies, it often feels like the end of the world. Suddenly and irreversibly, life, as we knew it, has ended. Things will never be the same. Plans for the future have vanished beneath the waves, hope evaporated in the heat of adversity, and any rations of self-confidence and courage we once had are in short supply.

Because grief books on the shelves of bookstores seldom look beyond the space between the tide pool and the breakers (the first six to twelve months or so after the loss,) I've never been much of a fan of them. They rarely look to the horizon. If they did, they'd realize that having lost one's mooring, many unsuspecting mourners have been flung far out to sea. Out there in the middle of nowhere without their captain or first mate, with no wind in their sails and no land in sight, they wonder, "What am I going to do now?" "Where do I go from here?" "How will I survive this?" "When is this grief going to end?" "Why didn't God answer my prayers?" "Who will be there for me in my time of need?" "Will I find love again?" and even, "What's the point of going on?" Time by itself answers none of these questions. It takes months, and possibly years of wondering and wandering to find answers and chart a new course in life. And, if you want to get out of this current predicament, on occasion you will have to pick up your oars and row.

This is not one of those self-help books that promise to help you resolve your grief in ten easy steps. Nor will you find within these pages the secret to decoding the map to the next phase of your life. What I can offer is insight; reflections from the experience of sitting in that tide pool, listening to the stories of people who have met their dragons and lived to tell the tale.

In part one of this book, you are going to meet three characters: Mico, Pete, and Peggy. They are composites of people I have known, not actual persons. I have created them for two reasons: First, because it is unethical to use an individual's personal story without their permission, even for such a noble purpose as to illustrate my points. Second, I have heard many stories similar to the ones I'm about to tell. These characters represent archetypes for all sorts of people who have experienced one type of loss or another. So, just for the sake of clarity, any similarity that you may see in my narrative to someone we may know in common is merely a coincidence.

Each of these characters struggle with life transition after loss and discover that dragons are not by nature malevolent— they might actually be appearing in challenging times to serve as our guardians and guides. Mico's encounter helps him find a new purpose in life. Pete wrestles with the unfairness of it all. And Peggy is finally able to accept the mantle of adulthood.

In the following pages, I'll share with you a few things I've learned from working with dragons, loss, and life transitions. For example, I've discovered that rituals are the single most effective way to charm a dragon. Today, ritual creation is almost a lost art. I think we began to set them aside when we finished mapping the globe, when we harnessed electricity, when we discovered penicillin—all important developments, but until we've conquered death, ritual will continue to be the best way to live with mystery. Rituals allow us to transcend space and time; they connect us when we feel isolated and alone. They can also create movement whenever we feel stalled or stuck; they put wind in our sails. It may be that you have not given much thought to rituals; I want to make the case for why you should give them a try.

I have been asked if I believe that dragons are real and not just metaphors. I can't say I've actually met one (at least that I can recall,) but that does not mean they don't exist. No doubt, such an encounter would be a life-altering experience! In part two of this book I've included three short stories where I imagined what an encounter with a dragon might be like. You will meet Lóng (pronounced, Loong), the Chinese water dragon who appears to Mico, Peggy, and Pete at a critical moment in their life transition after loss. Each story fills in a few more details about the challenges these characters faced and offers me the chance to illustrate some of the same questions from a slightly different angle.

I hope that this book provides, in a slightly unconventional way, what can happen when the waves of grief have carried you into parts unknown. Those old mapmakers may have been correct: beyond here there may be dragons, but that doesn't mean we can't be friends with them. Enough with introductions. All ashore who's going ashore—an adventure awaits!

Beyond Here There Be Dragons

PART ONE

1 BEYOND HERE THERE BE DRAGONS

There is a Chinese parable about a farmer who owned a horse that he used to help him plow his fields. One day, the horse ran away. The farmer's neighbors gathered to sympathize with him over his bad luck. The farmer responded to their concerns by saying, "Maybe bad, maybe good, I don't know." The next day, the horse returned bringing with it a herd of wild horses. His neighbors gathered to celebrate his good fortune. His reply to them was, "Maybe good, maybe bad, I don't know." When the farmer's son was attempting to tame one of the wild horses, he fell off and broke his leg. Everyone thought this was very bad. The farmer said, "Who's to say? It may be bad, it may be good, I don't know." The next day, the army marched into the village and conscripted every able-bodied young man into service—all except the farmer's son with the broken leg. Now, was that good or bad? Who can say?

I am inclined to agree with the Chinese farmer's perspective. I'm not a silver-lining guy, as in, "Every cloud must have its silver lining." I don't think something good has to come out of every situation. Sometimes a tragedy is simply a tragedy, and the negatives may far outweigh any meaningful or identifiable gain. The people who come to grief support groups relay stories of fumbled attempts at consolation like, "God never gives us more than we can handle," or, "Look on the bright side, she isn't suffering anymore." While well intentioned and possibly even true, these are not the kinds of things you want to say to someone whose loved one has just been diagnosed with a life-threatening illness or has just died from a sudden accident or a long, drawn-out disease.

William Bridges, an author and expert in the field of life transitions, recalled an exchange he had with his wife, Mondi, as she struggled with a diagnosis of breast cancer and the subsequent after-effects of surgery, radiation, and chemotherapy. "'This positive-thinking stuff is crap,' she said to me one evening as I sat on her hospital bed. 'But then, so is negative thinking. They both cover up reality, which is that we just don't know what is going to happen. That's the reality we have to live with. But it is easy to see why people take refuge in optimism or pessimism. They both give you an answer. But the truth is that we just don't know. What a hard truth that is!'"

One of the biggest challenges of any loss or life transition is learning how to deal with this hard truth. Families living with a chronic or life-threatening illness have to live with this reality, and so do those who have experienced the death of a loved one. Across our lifespan, we can also include the uncertainty surrounding moving to a new place, graduating from high school or college, getting married or starting a family, and starting or losing a job. In fact, none of us can say with any certainty what tomorrow will bring.

When I think about life transitions, an anthropologist named Arnold van Gennep comes to my mind. He studied this issue, and in 1909 he published a helpful book entitled *The Rites of Passage*. In it, he used the term "liminal" (a word that suggests crossing over a threshold) to describe when the circumstances of life cast a person into a nebulous, in-between zone, when one phase of life has ended and the next phase has yet to begin. Van Gennep observed that although rites of passage may differ across cultures, most seem to involve three movements.

The first movement is what he calls the pre-liminal stage. It involves *rituals of separation* that mark the end of one of the phases of life. I think the clearest examples of rituals of separation are those that mark the end of childhood. In many tribal societies, at an appointed time of the year, the elders physically separate adolescent girls and boys from their families and the community to instruct them in the ways of adulthood. As harsh as it sounds, adolescent boys, in particular, would sometimes be cast out in the wilderness alone in order to demonstrate they are old enough to survive on their own and take on the responsibilities of adulthood.

The second movement—the liminal stage—involves *rituals of transition.* Having crossed the threshold between everything that was familiar and uncharted territory, sometimes called the liminal zone, the person in transition has lost their identity and status within the community; they no longer belong. In transition, they are exposed and vulnerable to all sorts of dangers. They may have been given a blessing or amulet for protection, and possibly a weapon to aid their survival. They may have to accomplish a task, engage in purifying rituals, or acquire secret wisdom before they can return.

The third movement—the post-liminal stage— involves *rituals of reincorporation* that celebrate the successful completion of a challenge or a safe return to the community. These final rituals might include a public sharing of what happened on their epic journey, and the giving of something that signifies their new status in the community.

In contemporary America, funeral rites and memorial services (now often rebranded as "Celebrations of Life") focus primarily on the person who died. Beyond the meal that follows the burial or the scattering of ashes, there is a recognizable absence of mourning rituals designed specifically to support the loved ones left behind. More recently, another anthropologist, Ronald Grimes, suggested, "Our definition of death rites must be large enough to include not only ritualized preparations for death and rites performed near the time of death but also ritual activities that follow long after the occasion of a person's death."

Historically, those "ritual activities that follow long

after death," would have been part of a formal mourning period that typically lasted a year or more. However, in Western cultures, attitudes toward death, dying, and bereavement began to shift after World War I, and many mourning customs started to diminish or disappeared entirely.

Today, mourners are advised that "the best thing to do is keep busy," and thereby avoid those distressing and unpredictable waves of emotions. After a three-day bereavement leave, we are all expected to get right back to work. Supervisors and coworkers will offer obligatory expressions of sympathy for the loss, but the bereaved are expected to maintain their composure in public and quickly return to functioning at pre-loss levels.

Most people in our culture simply do not know what to say; either they mumble through a few awkward words of consolation or offer you some tired old cliché. Others are afraid they might say the wrong thing, so they choose to error on the side of saying nothing at all!

Well-meaning friends and neighbors promise their ongoing support: "If you need anything, just call ..." But, they quickly return to their own concerns and forget that grief continues for a protracted period of time.

In the absence of rituals and people to support the bereaved through this difficult life transition, they are (like refugees) set adrift upon the troubled waters of grief.

To complicate matters even more, there is nothing telling us how long grief and the mourning period should last. If it were officially over in six, twelve, or eighteen months, then there might be some sort of ritual of reincorporation at the end, a ceremonial announcement that the mourning period is officially over and the bereaved person has returned to share their insights and stories of survival.

Today, grief educators are reluctant to talk about loss in terms of universal stages or time frames, and instead, they emphasize that the bereaved should be allowed to define their own personal grief journey. The unintended consequence of this means that they are often left with few culturally defined indicators that help to facilitate movement through the life transition that inevitably follows a loss.

The people who come to see me for grief counseling say they feel lost and just don't know where to turn. The world as they know it has come to an end. Because society offers no clear direction, they come seeking a map of sorts that will guide them through their grief. I know some are hoping that I will give them a shortcut to help them "get through this as quickly as possible!"

The truth is that there aren't any shortcuts, nor is there one right way to go about it. The truth, even for seasoned travelers, is that these waters of grief are, for each of us, uncharted territory. The hard truth, as Mondi Bridges suggests, is we don't know what the future looks like or how long the journey is going to take. We all have to chart our own way, and every possible course we might choose will lead to a different future.

I fear that these truths I've spoken so far may lead the fainthearted to give up, abandon ship, or worse, refuse to ever leave the safety of the harbor. For the majority, for good or ill, there is no choice; that ship has set sail a long time ago. I've heard that mapmakers of old used to write at the edges of maps, "Beyond here there be dragons," leaving the reluctant mariner with the all-important question, "Dragons, perhaps, but are they friendly?"

2 MAKING FRIENDS WITH DRAGONS

In addition to rites of passage, anthropologists have collected creation stories from cultures across the globe. There are interesting similarities here as well. In the West, we are probably most familiar with the creation accounts found in the book of Genesis. We are told that on the second day of creation, God created the dome of the sky by separating the waters. It was in these primordial waters that dragons (chaos personified) first took their shape. In the Christian scriptures, especially in the book of Revelation, dragons are associated with the destructive power of chaos, fire, and the devil. Consequently, we tend to fear and do whatever we can to steer clear of them. In Job and Amos, in the Psalms, and in Isaiah there is a mythical dragon-like monster that lives in the sea called Leviathan. While in some instances the reference may simply refer to a whale, in other cases the name evokes the image of some kind of mysterious behemoth whose shape and ferociousness is best left only to the imagination.

In Eastern cultures, however, dragons are viewed more favorably. In Chinese mythology, dragons symbolize the more positive and creative side of chaos: power, generativity, and good luck. To be associated with dragons is considered most auspicious, a good omen, fortunate, and an indication of future success. Interestingly, unlike their Western fire-breathing cousins, in China, dragons have dominion over water in all its forms: oceans, rivers, storms, and floods. That said, seafarers, and others who find themselves in uncharted waters, would be well advised to learn a thing or two about dragons.

It is important to know that dragons, unpredictable creatures that they are, can never be completely tamed or controlled. However, I would like to believe that it is possible to make friends with them. The following are a few thoughts I have about how to deal with dragons, as well as life transitions.

1. Patience

As with many things, patience is the first requirement. We Westerners aren't very good at patience. We live in a culture that is all about instant gratification. The challenge is to learn how to tolerate the not-knowing, the in-between time, the liminal, the "not yet." It requires the ability to self-soothe, to calm yourself when you get frustrated or frightened. As you work with dragons and all the other things that scare you, you have to remind yourself to slow down and breathe. Admittedly, patience is a tough one, so it's best to practice patience in small bits. It also requires a certain degree of perseverance, so keep trying. ·

2. Courage

Dragons can smell fear like a shark can detect blood in water. However, when I speak of courage, I am not talking about a Saint-George-the-Dragon-Slayer kind of courage, but the kind that sees a challenge as an opportunity. The Latin root of the word courage is *cor* (heart). I would like to suggest that the *age* part suggests a sort of internal fortitude that comes through lived experience. To face your dragons, you have to believe in yourself, realize that you have been through some tough times in the past, and recognize that you will learn how to stand and confront the challenges in front of you as well. You have to be willing to put your heart out there, knowing full well that it could get hurt again. It takes courage to engage the world without that special someone, and determination to keep moving forward despite not knowing what the future has in store.

3. Move

I am not advising you to sell your house. What I mean by "move" is to accept the dragon's invitation to go for a walk on deck every day. Just as ships are built to be sailed, dragons and people need to move. Staying cooped up inside all day long would drive anybody, including a dragon, crazy! Much of the real work in life transitions involves an internal journey. However, an examination of all those rites of passage suggests that movement within can be facilitated by a willingness to expose oneself to the elements outside. By carefully observing the beauty of nature and the patterns of life, we begin to see this death, this loss, and this ending, in the context of some larger scheme.

4. Compass

Birds and butterflies, whales and dragons—all have an internal compass. In times of transition, with the sky dark and overcast, we would do well to follow their lead and access our own orienting systems. It might be that feeling you get in your gut, or extra sensory perception (ESP). It might be your unfailing faith in human resilience and ingenuity, or an abiding trust in, what people in twelve-step programs refer to as, "the God of your understanding." These are the types of resources we rely on when we're on the lookout for dragons, when we can't see in the dark, and when we have lost our way or been led astray.

5. Companions

While it is true that we are each on our own journey, I would like to think that we are never really completely alone. There are people and places where we can stop to rest and find shelter from the storm. It is often the case that the person who died was your captain or rowing partner, and the friends and family members you thought would be there quietly drift away. Realize that it is going to take time to develop new relationships. So, when you encounter a fellow sojourner, introduce yourself and ask him or her, "Ahoy, Matey. Have you seen any dragons?"

6. Food

Never feed a dragon, that is, unless you want it to get bigger and stronger. Dragons can take care of themselves. It is you who needs to focus on good nutrition. You will need every ounce of strength you can get for this long and arduous voyage. Think of things that will nourish your body, mind, and spirit. The smell of bread baking and the taste of homemade soup, a yoga class, a massage, or curling up with an afghan and a good book on a rainy Sunday afternoon are just some of the ways to refuel. A bit of dark chocolate on occasion doesn't hurt either. To indulge in a few comforting or tasty things once in a while when you grieve is not selfish; it is actually self-care.

7. Generosity

Helping others is good for the soul. People who volunteer have learned this important secret to happiness. I am not suggesting you have to formally volunteer; you can babysit for grandkids, sweep the neighbor's walk, or leave a little extra cash each time you tip. When we are wounded, the temptation is often to withdraw or lash out. While understandable, it neither satisfies nor soothes. Realize that dragons, like people, respond better to kindness. So be kind. Lavish forgiveness on the undeserving, compliment the lady in front of you in the checkout line for her excellent choice in attire, turn the other cheek, and when pressed into service, be willing to go the extra mile.

8. Music

A 17th century English playwright, William Congreve, wrote, "Music hath charms to soothe a savage breast, to soften rocks, or bend a knotted oak." It also works its powerful magic on dragons. Music resonates within us at a deeper level and vibrates across time, space, and cultures. It speaks, perhaps, the only language that a grieving and frightened heart can understand. My advice is to make music or listen to music. Sing. If you can't sing, try reading poetry out loud. In addition to music, I suggest looking for beauty found in nature and in all the creative arts. Dancing like a sailor is also highly recommended.

9. Humor

You might be surprised to learn that nothing endears you to a dragon more than to provide them with the opportunity for a hearty belly laugh. Dragons never take themselves (or anything else) too seriously, and they love to play keep-away and hide-and-go-seek. It will be immensely helpful for you to learn (or relearn) how to be playful. Seek out things that make you laugh, and for goodness' sake, don't take everything so seriously. There is absolutely no reason why people who grieve have to be so somber all the time. Realize that you are going to make some mistakes; it's not the first time and it certainly won't be the last, so ease up on yourself a little. No one can say how long it will take for you to chart a new course through this life transition. And yet, no matter how long it does take, if you are able to laugh (especially at yourself) then you will soon discover the journey is much more manageable.

10. Love

Finally, I'd like to suggest that dragons really aren't so scary once you get to know them. They can also serve as guardians to the wounded and vulnerable part of ourselves. We should learn to love them. The poet Rainer Maria Rilke, a contemporary of van Gennep, offered the following thought in *Letters to a Young Poet*: "Perhaps all the dragons in our lives are princesses who are only waiting to see us act, just once, with beauty and courage. Perhaps everything that frightens us is, in its deepest essence, something helpless that wants our love."

3 DRAGONS THRIVE IN CHAOS

For the moment, and possibly for the foreseeable future, the challenge before you is to learn how to survive, to live with and in the void for an extended period of time. I offer just one note of caution: do not make the liminal zone your home. Dragons thrive in chaos; humans, not so much.

Our early ancestors understood that rituals are a form of magic that can bring order to chaos, and in this situation, charm dragons. When considering what rituals might help you, I think it can be helpful to ask the question, "What can I do to calm these dragons?"

Something happened to our collective sense of ritual—the reasons for which, I'm certain I do not fully understand. No doubt in some people's minds, rituals are equated with mindless habit or monotonous routine. Others simply dismiss them as nothing more than superstition. Still others have been too quick to abandon them because the resulting effects cannot be monetized or are not always immediately perceived. Additionally, when the specialists we employ perform them scrupulously, sloppily, or self-servingly, there can be little doubt why those assembled leave hungry, frustrated, and bored. Lest we be too quick to find the fault in others, I need to remind you that ritual enactment was never intended to be a spectator sport.

Victor Turner, another anthropologist and the man credited with pulling van Gennep's concept of liminality out of the archives and applying it to modern society, also added a lot to the conversation about how rituals help facilitate passage from one state to another. I like his use of the phrase "betwixt and between" to describe the ambiguity felt, especially by the bereaved, who often say they don't know who they are anymore and feel like they no longer belong. Rituals can be thought of as a kind of lubricant that allows people to move through life transition more smoothly. For those who find themselves stranded seemingly in the middle of nowhere, I suggest that you think of ritual activity as hoisting the sails to catch the winds of change.

Many of the rituals we use today have evolved over the millennia and have survived the test of time precisely because they remain potent. I imagine when most people think of rituals, they usually think of the ones that involve incense and chanting for hours, or that require engaging the services of a priestess, shaman, or guru. If those rituals are meaningful to you, by all means, take advantage of them.

Access to new rituals is complicated. Today, many people are only loosely connected to the religious and cultural traditions of their forbearers. Consequently, they may not be familiar with (or interested in) the rituals that sustained the generations that preceded them.

Living in a society rich in cultural diversity and easy access to information presents its own challenges. A simple Internet search allows us to dip our toes into colorful and exotic rituals far different than our own. The downside is that in order for the rituals to be most effective, you really need to be immersed in the culture that created them, and unfortunately, we are seldom able or willing to dive beneath the surface.

In the absence of finding existing rituals, we can always invent our own. Rituals don't have to be pious or ancient in order to work; you can be serious or lighthearted, whimsical or solemn. I give you permission to have fun with writing your own rules.

When designing rituals, think in terms of two things: 1)

24

structure and 2) creativity. All rituals have a beginning, middle, and end. They typically involve some sort of movement (bowing, kneeling, processing, dancing,) and engage multiple senses (the smell and sight of incense rising, the taste of bread and wine, or the feeling of sand or grass beneath your bare feet.) Consider incorporating one of the natural elements (earth, air, fire, and water) into the ritual acts you perform. Ritual creation involves a willingness to suspend rationality. Abandon your inhibitions, your self-consciousness, and your judgmental and perfectionist tendencies. Be creative. Who cares if people are watching!

Here are some examples of rituals of transition for those who find themselves in the liminal zone:

- Enfold yourself in a loved one's jacket or robe after first sprinkling it with their favorite perfume or cologne.
- Did your father ever pass on a bit of personal wisdom or a favorite quote? Have it engraved (or tattooed) somewhere, and repeat it often.
- I bet your mother cooked the best _____. Try to replicate her recipe each year on her birthday or on a holiday. Reminisce with those who gather about how hers was the best.
- Light a candle at your place of worship or at home on his or her birthday or death anniversary/yahrzeit.
- Take part in Memorial Day, All Saints/Souls Day; attend a Yizkor service; or create your own special, annual day of remembrance.
- Visit important places associated with the person who died. Take pictures, leave something behind (ashes, a candle, a flower, or a stone.)
- Ask for a blessing or offer a blessing.
- Feed the birds or plant a garden and watch it grow.
- Donate annually to their favorite charity as a way to honor the person who died.

Rituals can also help us create movement in other areas of life where we feel stalled or stuck. It may be that there are aspects of your history with the one who died that were never addressed or resolved while they were living, or words that you wish you could take back or never had the chance to say. Certain residual emotions can hang like an anchor around your neck. Imagine what a ritual of forgiveness or reconciliation might look like. Visualize what it would be like to finally cut loose that thing that weighs you down, and then to feel the release once you are ultimately free.

There is one more aspect to ritual that is important to know. It may be the final piece needed to convince the reluctant mariner to go ahead and give them a go. Rituals are always about relationship. They connect us, even when we are alone—especially when we are alone. The liminal zone can be vast, as it exists outside space and time. There is no past, no future; there is only the eternal *here*, the eternal *now*. Rituals show us that labels like *the living* and *the dead* are distortions, not distinctions. Rituals allow us to grab hold of an invisible strand that, when followed to its end, bind all into the One.

Elaborate and long, or short and sweet, a ritual can be performed once or repeated as often as needed. They can be spontaneous or scripted, done alone or acted out with others. Whatever rituals you choose to do, when completed, always ask the dragon, "How did that make you feel?" If the answer is at least "a little bit better," then I'd say it was a success.

Thomas John Dennis

4 WRESTLING WITH DRAGONS

Rituals have the power to charm the dragons we encounter, but by themselves are not enough to get us where we need to go. Those silver one-liners make it sound so easy. "Time heals," they say as if all you need to do is batten down the hatches and endure the squall. Anyone who has been through the liminal zone will tell you that kind of passive thinking will get you nowhere at all. Yes, coping with loss and life transition will take time, but it also requires real effort.

Before Pete's wife was diagnosed with cancer, he was struggling with a career move he had recently made. He left the company he'd been working for since college, enticed to a new start-up that by all accounts promised a brighter future, not to mention a much bigger salary. As is sometimes the case, the grass wasn't greener on the other side. Sure, the money was great, but along with the bigger salary came bigger headaches and much longer hours.

When his wife started chemo, his new boss (twenty years his junior), was hardly sympathetic. It was a vastly different experience from his previous boss (the grandson of the company founder), who always treated all his employees like family. After his wife died, Pete felt like a ship without a rudder. Personally, and professionally, he felt completely lost. He dreaded getting up in the morning and going through the motions day after day, after day.

Still a few years from retirement, his future appeared

bleak. When he and his wife had dreamed of retiring, they planned to go on a cruise, see the world, spend time with the grandkids, and take care of each other in their old age. So much for that vision of their golden years.

Pete wrestled for quite a while with what to do. Initially, it was hard to accept the reality that she was actually gone. Then he tried to push through it, as many men (and a fair number of women) try to do.

When that no longer worked, he tried alcohol for a while. To his good fortune, it was soon after that he happened to meet Mico, an old tattooed fisherman, in an all-night diner.

Mico, himself a widower, listened compassionately to Pete's concerns. He admitted to Mico that when his wife died, it felt like a cannonball ripped through his mid-deck and he was left alone to piece together the remnants of their shattered dreams.

"Life wasn't supposed to happen this way," Pete complained. "We had a plan! Now everywhere I look, all I see is collateral damage. With her it was always smooth sailing, life had meaning ... but not anymore."

"When she died," he went on to say, "I lost my reason to get up in the morning and my reason to come home at night. She was my sunshine, my moral compass, my first mate."

One thing he hadn't lost was a group of family and friends who remained supportive long past what I call "the shallows." As time passed, after Pete entered the deepest part of the ocean, some of those friends eventually drifted off in other directions, but a few remained steadfastly beside him. At the lead of his personal flotilla was old Mico.

Having been through the liminal zone himself, Mico was able to help Pete gain some perspective. In addition to listening to Pete without judgment, he offered a few ideas by sharing what worked for him. It was Mico who encouraged Pete to, "Just go talk to your old boss, and see what he has to say."

When Pete finally mustered up the courage to speak with his old boss, he was welcomed back to the company as if he were the prodigal son. His boss said he couldn't match the same salary as that new start-up, but Pete didn't mind.

Returning to his previous job was as easy as slipping into an old pair of shoes. Feeling more comfortable about his present situation, Pete wrestled again with what his future would look like. "When you are ready," his friends and an occasional coworker would say, "I can fix you up with a really nice widow—or divorcée."

Pete didn't think being fixed up was going to fix anything. It was not as if a new relationship was the solution to mending his rended heart. Pete was grateful for their concern but would politely mumble that he didn't think he was ready for that just yet.

"To be totally honest," Pete told Mico one night at the diner, "I know it's not possible, but I just want my wife back, along with the future we planned together."

Mico pointed out, "You can still spend time with the grandkids, and there is no reason why you can't travel."

Pete agreed about the grandkids, "They are my one source of joy. And yes, I can find people to travel with. I can also afford to pay the single supplement, but that's not the point. The point is, we were supposed to travel *together*! Without her," he wondered aloud, "what's the point?"

Eventually, Pete came to realize that it had taken them years to carefully construct their dreams, and as Mico noted, "Realistically, it will probably take a couple more years to jury-rig a new future out of the pieces that are left."

(Historical note: The term "jury-rig," was originally a naval term. It describes any kind of makeshift device built out of whatever you can find. I guess when you are out in the middle of the ocean with no land in sight, you have to get creative to find your way out of the current predicament.)

Once Pete was able to accept that reality, the dark clouds on the horizon seemed much less ominous. And the emotional fog inside Pete also began to lift. People around him commented on the change they could see in him. Less anxious and less depressed, Pete actually began to look forward to the start of each new day, excited about the possibilities it might bring.

Pete's dragon took many forms, but his biggest challenge was to wrestle with imagining, and then constructing, a future without the love of his life.

Time, without real effort on your part, will get you nowhere; it only makes you old. If you seriously want to get through this life transition, you are going to have to grab hold of the tail of an idea, a dream, a hope, or a dragon, and hang on!

Thomas John Dennis

5 THE DRAGON'S MARK

You may be familiar with the story of another man (this one named Jacob) who, on his way home one day, was forced to wrestle at the water's edge with a mysterious stranger. We are told that, despite an injury that left him limping for life, Jacob refused to release his hold. When the stranger realized that Jacob would never let go, he asked, "What is your name?" Jacob told him. The mysterious stranger then blessed him and said, "Your name shall no longer be Jacob, but Israel [a Hebrew word meaning, *to have the power of a prince*], for you have struggled with God and with men, and have prevailed."

If Rilke is right, and dragons really are princesses (or princes) just waiting to see us act, just once, with beauty and courage, then wrestling with and befriending them will certainly be empowering. Dragons always bless their friends with gifts—gifts less tangible perhaps than silver, but certainly more valuable than gold.

Sometimes they gift us with a little nudge or a puff of wind to fill our sails, taking us in a new direction. For those who can't go home, it is on to a new adventure, a new love interest, or a new purpose in life. After all, there are islands out there—interesting people to meet and exotic lands yet to see. When traveling in the company of a dragon, what once seemed impossible or frightening, is now much less so. Survivors of the gales of grief have gone on to do some amazing things.

They have built monuments, endowed educational and medical initiatives, and started charitable foundations. Out of the wreckage of loss, new visions and new dreams have emerged.

At other times, what the dragon gives us is a magical ruby-slipper-like return ticket home. Those who have come back and shared their epic saga of loss and life transition describe how they have changed. They say they no longer see the world the same way as before. They don't sweat the small stuff (as much.) They are more intentional about telling the people they love that they are loved. They say they are less sure about a lot of things, but they are better at being okay with everything not always having to be okay. They develop a knack for finding beauty in the most unexpected places.

While I would never wish profound grief upon anyone, what I know is that when we reflect on the experience of loss and the life transition that follows, there are some potential gifts for those who are open to receiving them. We learn what empathy and compassion really mean. The experience stirs within us a profound sense of gratitude for the small kindnesses offered in a moment of need. It compels us to learn new skills that we can take pride in, and introduces us to friends we have not yet met. It invites us to explore the deepest part of the ocean as we search for answers to life's biggest questions.

Here's an example of one gift that I hear about quite regularly in the grief support groups I facilitate for adults who have lost a parent: At the diner where Mico and Pete frequently meet, there is a waitress named Peggy. She really likes Mico because he's always so cheerful and kind, not to mention a generous tipper. Shortly after her mother died, Peggy confided to Mico that she felt like it was, "finally time to grow up."

Her statement may have surprised van Gennep. In contrast to tribal societies, here in the modern world there is no real clearly defined end to adolescence. There are still religious rites that function as rites of passage, such as a bar/bat mitzvah or confirmation, but the delay in taking on the full responsibility of adulthood continues well beyond the completion of rituals like these. Secular events like getting a driver's license, graduating from high school or college, starting your first real job, marriage, or even having children, incrementally push us towards adulthood but do not necessarily compel us to mature developmentally.

Very often, it is only after the death of the second parent that adult daughters and sons say they feel like they finally have to "step up," or "grow up." As long as one parent is alive, we can maintain the fantasy that death might not come for us. After they die, we are confronted with the reality that, "Oh my gosh, I could be next!" Nothing makes a person grow up faster than this sobering thought.

Peggy went on to tell Mico, "Somehow, just having her around made the world feel like a safer place. She was the last of her generation. Now that she's gone, the kids are looking to me for answers, but I don't think I'm ready for that." Her mother had been the matriarch of the family, and everyone agreed that nobody could fill her shoes. Ready or not, Peggy suddenly found herself face to face with a dragon, and it was, to say the least, disconcerting.

Over the months that followed, on those occasions when Mico stopped in the diner, Peggy would seek out his advice. Usually he'd point her somewhere that would help expand her circle of support, like joining a grief support group or going to talk to her mother's priest. Every once in a while, he'd also loan her a book on the subject that he'd found helpful. "There is no shortage of sages from across the ages," he'd say. "You're not the first person to struggle with these questions; somebody out there has got to have a plausible answer, I'm sure of it."

Rilke, for example, also tendered this sage advice in his *Letters to a Young Poet*, and I think it too applies pretty well to all of life's transitions: "Be patient toward all that is unresolved in your heart and try to love the questions themselves, like locked rooms and like books that are written in a very foreign tongue. Do not now seek the answers, which cannot be given you because you would not be able to live them. And the point is, to live everything. Live the questions now. Perhaps you will then gradually, without noticing it, live along some distant day into the answer."

However, the most helpful thing Mico did was just ask Peggy one simple question: "What would your mother have done in this situation?" Eventually it dawned on Peggy that it wasn't so much what her mother said, it was more the way she left you with the sense that, no matter what happens in life, "I love you, I'm so proud of you, we'll figure this out together."

Peggy also realized, "Mom didn't always get it right, so I figure that I'm allowed to make a few mistakes of my own. Forget filling Mom's shoes," she told Mico. "I donated them all to charity a long time ago, but …" Patting her shoulders, she continued, "The mantle of adulthood seems to be fitting pretty well these days. Or, at the very least, now I'm thinking it is something that I can grow into."

There are other things we can take from our encounters with dragons that ultimately you will have to discover on your own. Turner suggested that encounters with what he refers to as "monsters" startle us into thinking about aspects of our life that we have up until this point taken for granted. He goes on to say, "During the liminal period neophytes are alternately forced and encouraged to think about their society, their cosmos and the power that generates and sustains them. Liminality may be partly described as a state of reflection." Perhaps that's one reason why the life transition that follows loss takes so long.

Peggy's story points us to one important lesson to ponder on those starry nights when you lie sleepless on a glassy sea. Death is the great equalizer; it happens to the rich and the poor. The same sun sets on the good and the bad alike. This hardest of truths is also the thing that connects us to all living things. None of us is going to get out of here alive. Instead of spending so much time and energy trying to avoid death, should we not instead dedicate ourselves to the principle of making every moment count?

Having wrestled with dragons and navigated the

unknown, like Peggy, you too have been changed. Limping, or perhaps a little worse for wear, you have survived and you have been blessed. Or at least, you will be ...

How do you know you are emerging from the liminal zone and that it's time to move forward or go home?

At some point, the people I work with will say something like, "I can't quite put my finger on it, but it feels like some kind of shift has taken place." They're often quite tentative about saying it, and understandably so; more often than not, emergence from a life transition happens gradually, sporadically, and unevenly, like winter turning into spring.

It also seems entirely possible that a number of these shifts need to occur before a person can say with any degree of certainty that they have crossed the boundary between what life used to be and whatever it eventually becomes. Very often it is only in retrospect that a person can declare with confidence that they are "done."

6 LAND HO!

Human beings are born with limbs, not fins. We are land animals. The ocean is not our home. As you emerge from the liminal zone and terra firma is within your sight, pause for a moment with me so I can share with you one more hard truth. You might be thinking that this is the time when you finally get to take a deep breath and quietly relax into the next phase of your life, but unfortunately, you'd be wrong. Sorry that I have to be the one to tell you, but you are not there yet.

Even when you successfully emerge from this transition, it does not follow that you will be done with grief. Whereas transitions take from months to years, from my perspective, the waves of grief will rise and fall episodically throughout your life. This hard truth is the "bitter" part of "bittersweet."

You will revisit this and other losses countless times over the remainder of your life journey. Memories trigger emotions both happy and sad. On birthdays and anniversaries, on holidays, weddings, and graduations, and on other special family occasions, you will experience what I call a "ripple" of grief. The good news is all those future ripples will not be as frequent or intense as the "waves" that washed over you previously.

There will be new losses and life transitions that can rush in and drag you out with the tide. On such occasions, you'll wish that special someone was with you to offer reassurance; you will miss them because you know they would know exactly what to do or say. You will reexamine this and other previous losses in the hope of salvaging whatever coping skills you can find in order to deal with what's next.

To grieve again later does not mean that you didn't grieve the first time, or that you somehow did it wrong. It simply means that over the course of life, you are given new opportunities to consider the lessons of love and loss again, from the perspective of an older and wiser you. All these later ripples and waves signify points on the journey where you stop and look back, then forward, and make an assessment of how you are doing at that particular moment in time. My hope is always that, from this new vantage point, you will be able to say something like, "Yes, I still miss him or her, but I'm doing okay." If you're not, the good news is that there are people—and dragons—willing to help if you ask.

Mico would be the first person to admit, "There isn't a day that goes by that I don't think of my wife." Then he is quick to add, "But I am no longer lost without her. In fact, these days I actively look for ways to pour out the love I have for her on others." What I think Mico is pointing to is the idea that it's not about simply "letting go" and "moving on," but rather finding meaningful and creative ways to "carry on" without that special someone steadfastly by your side.

We should not forget the "sweet" part of "bittersweet" either. Mondi Bridges was pretty critical of the folks who just have to find the silver lining no matter what. But, she found equal fault with those who filter everything through progressively darkening shades of gray. Negativity sucks the life out of any transition, and pessimism is a path that only leads to isolation. Believe me, you don't want to end up there.

Floating amongst the wreckage after loss, even a characteristically positive person can become soured to life. Afflicted with poor health, devastated by loss, or beset by a series of unfortunate events, who could blame anybody else for losing their appetite for life?

I concede that the world can be a dangerous place, that

bad things happen to good people, and that loved ones die and innocents suffer. What I refuse to do though, is sit at home and wait for dreadful things to occur. Who better than the inspirational author and activist Helen Keller to tell us that we must step boldly into life in order to truly live? She asserted, "Life is either a daring adventure or nothing at all. Security does not exist in nature, nor do the children of men as a whole experience it. Avoiding danger is no safer in the long run than outright exposure."

Life is not all bitterness and woe. It is a daring adventure that is, for you, not over yet. To taste its sweetness, you must cultivate curiosity and a willingness to try new things. Learn to wander, to linger longer. Stop rushing about! Look for the good, and laugh a lot. Practice gratitude in small things: a door opened, a well-turned phrase, the sound of wind in the leaves, this breath, this moment, and you will soon be tasting *la dolce vita*, the sweet life. Savor the flavor of everything!

7 THE HEART OF A DRAGON

To stride fearlessly into the day, knowing that there are no guarantees, requires the heart of a dragon. If you have gotten this far and gathered all these hard truths into your heart, you are ready. It is time to proceed.

Recall, van Gennep suggested that the third step in his rites of passage, *rituals of reincorporation*, typically involves some kind of public pronouncement or celebration upon one's return. Often they are given a tangible symbol of their new identity or newly defined role in the community. It might be a physical mark on the body, such as a dragon tattoo, or it could be investiture with a garment, pendant, or something symbolic of one's newly acquired status.

In our culture, there are no harbormasters, no guardians at the gate, no secret passwords to whisper upon your return. There are no ceremonies, no new garments, and unfortunately, there is no medal for courage awarded to the bereaved. There are no visible, physical marks that I'm aware of. In fact, most people may not have even noticed that you've been gone. Instead of any outward discernible indication, often what takes place is an internal, existential transformation.

In days of old, there were wisdom figures, village elders, who, having wrestled their own dragons, were willing to offer guidance to the newly initiated about ways to navigate in the liminal zone without losing hope.

Having successfully negotiated your way through the liminal zone, befriended a dragon, and come home or headed off to new adventures, you can for all intents and purposes consider yourself done with this particular life transition. You have earned a well-deserved respite from the chaos and a seat in the council of elders. If, however, like Mico, you are on occasion willing to consider wading into the waters of someone else's grief, then I have a proposal for you.

I'm recruiting for an armada of dragon-hearted warriors willing to sail the Seven Seas. There are castaways out there, exiles stranded by the storms of grief.

In the absence of culturally defined rites of passage and with few friends and acquaintances who truly understand, you are in a unique position to offer more than just silver one-liners to the bereaved. You've been there, done that, and are a living testament to the fact that it is possible to not only survive, but also, eventually, to thrive. You could be that kindly widow or widower across the alley, the compassionate stranger at the diner, or the old friend who remembers long after all others have forgotten.

There are lessons only someone who has been there can teach. Practical things, like how to spot a pirate, and the proper way to address a dragon once you finally get to meet one. While it is not within our power to still the chaos, nor is it our job to rescue the bereaved, nevertheless, we can help them get their bearings and offer them fresh water and supplies. As Mico says, "They may be slow to accept help from a stranger, but you can tell them that a burden shared by two is half as heavy, and any ship will ride higher when it carries a lighter load."

Nobody's army is going to march into town and draft you into service. What I'm organizing is a fleet of volunteers. If you accept my invitation, I have to tell you upfront that the hours can be long. While the pay is not great, I believe the freely offered gift of self is its own reward. All you have to do is keep a lookout, and when you encounter someone who appears lost, give them a shout, "Ahoy, Matey! There be dragons in these waters. Want to know what to do when you meet one?"

Thomas John Dennis

8 THE LAST HORIZON

One of those dragon-hearted warriors whose vision inspires me is Erik Erikson. He made it his life's work to help us understand human development across the lifespan. He argued that when we approach the end of our own journey with events like retirement, serious illness, and the death of friends and loved ones, we are challenged to ask some hard questions like:

What do I want to do with the time I have left?
Did I make a difference?
Was it all worth it?
Why me?
What's the point of prayer if the thing you pray for doesn't happen?
Do I still believe what I said I believed all these years?
Is there some kind of continued existence after death?
Will anyone miss me when I'm gone?

Those who are able to resolve these questions in a positive way will undoubtedly acknowledge some mistakes, but in the end, they will conclude life was a daring adventure well worth the trip. They are then able to complete their life journey with a sense of satisfaction, contentment, and peace. For example, Peggy's mother requested that a prayer composed by St. Teresa Benedicta of the Cross be printed on her Memorial Mass card. She said her mom used to pray it every day: "I cannot see very far ahead, but when I come to where the horizon closes down, a new prospect will open before me, and I shall meet it with peace."

Conversely, those whose past is littered with debris from a lifetime of conflict, failure, and disappointment, can wind up endlessly circling in a whirlpool of regret, bitterness, and despair. Sad but true. May this cautionary tale serve as a reminder while there is still some time to do something about it, so that their unfortunate ending will not be the same for you.

If you are lucky, over the course of your lifetime, you will have visited the liminal zone many times. "Lucky" in the sense that adversity tends to teach us more profound lessons than privilege does. Lucky, because coping skills are honed by hardship. Lucky, because in the end you realize that a person's true value is measured not in how much they acquired, but in what they gave away. If you are lucky, over the course of your lifetime, you will have visited the liminal zone many times so that when you face the final life transition, you need not be afraid. "Depending on your perspective, Heaven and Hell, reincarnation, conversion to cosmic energy, or nothingness, death is either the end of the journey or the beginning of a whole new adventure."

Although we will never know the rest of the story, I am betting that despite a broken leg, the Chinese farmer's son eventually got back up on that horse. One thing I do know is that in spite of a limp, Israel went on to become the father of a great nation. All of us one-eyed, peg-legged sailors (Rainer, Helen, St. Teresa, Mico, Pete, Peggy, you, and me,) we all have something in common: a noble and powerful friend who reigns with dominion over the waves of grief.

Time alone, in between what was and what is yet-to-be, is challenging, and the negatives may sometimes overshadow any meaningful or identifiable gain. The ones who give up too soon, or just "keep busy," will never obtain the heart of a dragon. But for those who dare to sail beyond their comfort zone, being empowered by a dragon is a definite possibility.

To associate with dragons is considered most

auspicious, an indicator of future success. While I remain suspicious of silver linings and maintain that we cannot know for certain what the future has in store, I know better than to give up hope for the possibility of a better future. Just because we cannot see beyond that dark horizon does not mean tomorrow offers no more brighter days!

Beyond Here There Be Dragons

PART TWO

THE TALE OF MICO AND THE DRAGON

He hooked his cane on the lip of the counter and eased himself up on the stool with a sigh. "Old bones," he said, while extending his hand to shake. "Name's Mico."

Startled by the abrupt introduction, Pete eyed with suspicion the man who just sat next to him. *He looks harmless enough, kind even,* Pete thought, and truth be told, he didn't mind the company. "Mine's Peter." He wiped his hand on a napkin and reached over, "But my friends call me Pete."

Mico's handshake was firm for an old guy. Pete guessed he was a fisherman. It wasn't a difficult deduction given the tattoos on Mico's forearms; that, and the fact that they were sitting in Bud's Diner, just one street over from the marina.

The waitress approached with a pot of coffee in hand. "How ya doin', Mico?"

Clearly he's a regular, Pete thought.

"I'm doing fine, Peggy, how are you?"

"Sunny-side up." (This was her quirky waitress way of saying, "I'm good.") "The usual?"

"Yes, my dear. And how is your mother?"

Peggy filled his cup without even breaking eye contact. "She's spunky as ever, Mom's already running that nursing home like she owns the place."

"Well, tell her I'll be stopping by on Tuesday, will ya?"

"Absolutely."

Turning her attention to Pete, she asked, "Can I get you anything else, sweetie?"

Pete smiled. "I could really use a piece of homemade pie—what do you recommend?"

"Peach, it's the only kind we have left."

"My favorite," Pete said, which was not a lie.

"Be right back with that." She winked at Mico as she walked away.

That's how Pete met the man who introduced him, indirectly, to a dragon. (But let's not get ahead of the story.) They talked long into the night. At some point, Pete and Mico moved into a booth to be more comfortable. Pete ended up spilling his guts to Mico, about how his wife had died, his frustration with work, his feelings of utter devastation, and his fears about the future. Mostly Mico just listened, nodding once in a while until Pete had managed to let it all out.

It suddenly occurred to Pete that while Mico now knew just about everything about himself, he knew next to nothing about Mico. "I'm sorry, I haven't given you a chance to talk much about yourself."

Mico shared his story of love and loss: He married his high school sweetheart and had a successful career in advertising, but at some point decided he didn't want the stress anymore, so they sold everything and moved to the coast. He bought a charter fishing boat and they lived happily ever after, until, well …

"After my wife, Jewell, died, I felt pretty lost. I drank a lot and didn't take my rig out for days and weeks at a time. My crew basically abandoned me, and I couldn't blame them— they had mouths to feed. At that point I was pretty much living on my boat because the house reminded me of her too much.

"One day I decided to take the boat out by myself. Only a damn fool does something like that. I didn't file a plan with the harbormaster, I didn't check to see how much diesel I had in the tank, and most importantly, I didn't check the weather. If I had, I would have found out there was a major squall working its way down the coast. But I was inconsolable, and if I had been honest with myself, I had no intention of doing any fishing.

"At about noon things started to change. I could see the clouds on the horizon and the sea itself started rolling, but I continued heading west. A voice inside told me to turn around, but I didn't listen. I just kept going further out to sea.

"As the sky progressively got darker, my intentions became clearer, I wanted to join my beloved, Jewell. The problem was, I was too much of a chicken to do it myself. I wanted the sea to take me."

Mico continued, "The storm was worse than you could ever imagine. The clouds were gray. The sea was black. The waves tossed my little boat around so much I could hardly tell which way was up. Imagine riding a roller coaster at midnight. That's pretty much what it felt like; only this ride had a very different ending. I was so disoriented, I lost all sense of time. Then the engine cut off. I knew I had to be out of fuel. I was totally at the mercy of the sea. It was right about then that I saw it."

"Saw what?" Pete asked, sitting on the edge of his seat, his hands clamped to the coffee cup as if holding on to the rail of Mico's boat.

"A dragon, of course."

Pete sat back. *Oh boy, an old fisherman spinning a yarn, and I bought the whole thing—hook, line, and sinker.*

"I know you don't believe me," Mico said. "I didn't believe it myself at first. I thought I was going crazy! I thought my eyes were playing tricks on me. Of course, it was dark out there. The only time you could see anything was when the lightning flashed. In the distance, I saw something in the clouds, but I couldn't quite make it out. One moment it was there, and the next it was gone. It looked a little bit like a massive snake weaving its way through the clouds; kinda stirring them up, so to speak.

"Just then my attention was pulled back to the water, to my port side, and all I could see was a wall of water headed straight for me. You're supposed to turn your boat into the wave, but with no power, I was totally screwed—pardon my French. It crashed on top of me like a ton of bricks. Next thing I knew, I was in the water. I thought I was a goner."

Mico took a sip of coffee. "Truth is, I didn't mind. The sea has swallowed untold numbers of sailors and fishermen over the years. No one would miss me, nobody would second-guess what I was doing out on a day like that—just another fisherman lost at sea. So, I simply 'let go.' I relaxed into the waves and let the water claim me. A strange calmness came over me at that point. As I was sinking down into the cold darkness, I knew it wouldn't be long before being reunited with my wife.

"It's a strange thing, death. We spend our whole lives trying to avoid it. But when you finally look it in the eye, you realize it's like stepping through a doorway. It's as simple as that. Oh, don't misunderstand me, dying is the hard part, but death, it's a release.

"Anyway, turns out I didn't die." Mico let out a short little laugh as if he still couldn't believe it himself. "The next thing I knew, something grabbed me and pulled me up and back onto the deck. I flopped around like a fish, choking and gasping for breath. And just before I passed out, exhausted and shivering, I heard a voice that said, 'Not today, Mico. Today is not your day to die.'"

Mico looked deep into the darkness of his coffee cup, and they sat silently for a while.

He continued, "The next day, I woke up in a daze. The sun was shining, the sea was calm, and there wasn't a ship or strip of land in sight. I checked the radio, and it didn't work. I tried to start the motor. It didn't turn over—no diesel, I remembered—and for some inexplicable reason, the compass and fancy navigational gizmos also didn't work. I couldn't have gone too far from the coast, could I?

"I must have been dreaming, I thought, or I bumped my head and got knocked out. I rubbed the back of my head—no bump. Clearly I was imagining things, right?"

Pete didn't know how to reply, so he just nodded his head kind of zigzaggedly.

"I felt a little embarrassed, a little ashamed for wanting to end it all, and look where that got me! 'Fine mess you've made of things Mico,' I said out loud. I instantly regretted my foolish, halfhearted suicide attempt. I realized that I never wanted to die, I just wanted the grief to end. I missed my precious Jewell desperately, and every night I ached with the desire to be reunited with her.

"I wondered how I managed to end up back in the boat? And what about the voice? Was it the voice of an angel? Was it God? Was my mind playing tricks on me? I looked up at the sky. It was bright and blue and beautiful—not a cloud in sight. 'Well,' I shouted to God or the universe or to whatever was listening, 'For what it's worth, thank you!' 'You're welcome,' came a response from above."

Mico looked Pete in the eye intently, "Now son, this is the point where most people say, 'You were hallucinating.' But honest to God, right there, six feet in front of me, a face materialized, a face like nothing I'd seen before. Its eyes were yellow, it had teeth like daggers, and horns that curved like the devil's himself. Hanging in the air, right in front of me like a kite, its tail whipping in the wind, was a huge dragon! Its scales glistened in the morning sun in shades of blue and green. I fell backwards onto the deck, stunned. It let out a huge laugh that shook the entire boat, and I'm not ashamed to say, I almost peed my pants I was so scared.

"It laughed again, only this time louder than before. 'That never gets old,' it said, with a certain degree of self-satisfaction in its voice, 'I love to see you humans' reactions when I do that! Ha, ha, ha.' Come to find out, dragons have a great sense of humor," Mico confided. Both Mico and Pete laughed at that.

The old guy's story was so captivating that from that point on, Pete was willing to suspend any sense of disbelief. Even though he knew dragons didn't exist, Pete realized he wanted this one to be real.

Mico asked with a tremble, "Are ... are you going to eat me?"

"If I were going to eat you," the dragon replied, "I would have done so last night."

"Then what are you going to do?"

"I am going to let you in on a little secret." The dragon paused for effect, then shared, "Life is hard—and then you die."

"Thanks," Mico said sarcastically. "I already figured that one out on my own."

"Let me finish," said the dragon. "Life is hard and then you die, but if you know how and where to look, there are treasures to be found."

"Once, I had a precious Jewell, but I lost her to cancer," Mico's voice cracked as he choked back tears.

"*What we have once enjoyed and deeply loved we can never lose,*" the dragon recited, "*for all that we love deeply becomes a part of us.*"

"*Didn't Helen Keller say that?*" Mico asked.

"*Yes, she did. One of my closest friends,*" the dragon said. "*Can you believe it?*"

"*I'm not sure what I believe anymore,*" Mico confessed. "*After all, at the moment, I happen to be talking to a dragon.*"

"*Point taken,*" the dragon said and turned as if to leave.

"*Wait!*" Mico called after him or her—he couldn't tell for sure. "*Don't go! You can't just leave me here ... I ... I don't even know your name.*"

The dragon turned around slowly. "*My name,*" said the dragon "*cannot be pronounced with a human tongue. To your ear it sounds a bit like rolling thunder, but you may address me by my Chinese name, Lóng.*"

"*Thank you Lóng,*" Mico said sincerely. "*I really mean it. I've realized I don't want to die ... I mean, I thought I did ... I just miss my wife so much.*"

"*You are welcome,*" Lóng said. "*Don't ever try something as foolish as that again!*"

"*I won't,*" Mico replied.

"*And as for the death of your mate, I offer my heartfelt condolences.*"

"*Thank you, again,*" Mico said.

"*I've seen my share of human suffering over the millenniums, and few losses match the death of a spouse in depth or degree.*"

"*Over the millenniums?*" Mico asked in amazement, "*How old are you?*"

"*I am as old as the sun,*" Lóng replied, "*and as young as today.*"

Mico wondered what that could possibly mean, but was afraid to ask. "*So where do you come from?*"

"*I come from the border between here and nowhere,*" Lóng said definitively.

Another cryptic answer. "*I see,*" Mico said, but he really didn't. "*Well then, could you at least tell me where I am, so that I can begin to figure out how to get back to where I'm from?*"

"*You,*" Lóng said, "*are in uncharted territory.*"

"*That's helpful,*" Mico replied with a hint of sarcasm.

"Mico," Lóng said somewhat forcefully, "where you go from here, either back to where you are from, or on to somewhere new, is up to you. Once you figure that out, I guarantee that how you will get there will no longer be a problem."

With that, Lóng turned and zipped away, stopping only momentarily to say, "I'll see you tomorrow."

———

Peggy came back and refilled their coffee. She didn't say a word; she sensed the depth of their conversation, and with her silence, communicated that they were welcome to stay and talk as long as needed.

"Mico," Pete asked tentatively, "I've got to ask, did Lóng come back?"

"Dragons always keep their word, Pete— Lóng came back the next day, and the next, and the next. All told I spent 137 days out there on the open ocean, and every day Lóng came back."

"So, what did you eat? How did you survive? What did you and Lóng talk about all those times?" Pete wondered aloud.

"Hold on, one question at a time," Mico said. "As for what I ate, I'm a fisherman, remember? And as for what we talked about, we talked about my wife a lot, or at least I did, and Lóng listened. Some days we explored deep questions: Is there an afterlife? How can a loving God allow innocent people to suffer? And what's the meaning of life? That kind of stuff. Lóng was a patient teacher, and like any good teacher, always made me propose a possible answer to my questions first. Then that damn dragon would respond with another one of those cryptic answers, and I would spend my nights staring up at the stars thinking about what it all meant."

"I know what you mean," Pete said to Mico, "I'm usually up half the night, my mind racing with questions, and none of my old answers seem to work anymore."

"Well, I do not recommend spending months at sea as the best way to solve the mysteries of life, but I do recommend consulting a dragon." The old fisherman smiled to himself. He went on, "I think it takes something bad like the death of a loved one, or some other kind of tragedy or natural disaster, to make us stop and reexamine our assumptions about the world and how things work. The good news is, every religion and philosophical system offers a response to each of those questions. You just have to take the time and make the effort to figure out which one makes the most sense to you."

"So, if you could share only one thing you learned during that time with Lóng, what would it be?" Pete asked.

Mico leaned back and paused for a brief moment to consider the question.

"Be generous."

"Okaaaay," Pete stretched the word out wanting more of an explanation, "what does that mean?"

"Look, at some point we all search for the answers to life's big questions, am I right? But the answers don't come overnight. You've got to work for them. In the meantime, be generous. That means be nice to people, even when they aren't always nice to you. Go out of your way to talk to a stranger in a diner who looks a little lost." He offered a sideways look, and Pete blushed a bit.

Mico continued, "Be patient at the intersection, wave the other car on through. What's so important that you can't take a few more seconds out of your day to be nice? Give to those less fortunate without counting the cost. You think you got it bad? Look around you for goodness' sake! Never take something from the land or the sea or the air without first giving thanks. More often than not, something has to die so that you can continue to live, so I challenge you to consider, what will you give back in return?"

"So, is this you or the dragon talking?" Pete interjected.

"A little bit of both, I'm sure. If Lóng had not been so generous with me, I might have drifted directionless for the rest of my miserable days, but by example Lóng gave me a new purpose, a new direction in life. My heart is no longer empty without my wife. I cultivate the love I still have for her by pouring it out onto others. And you know what happens when you are generous? Nine times out of ten, people offer themselves back in equal measure. We are all looking for the same thing, after all.

"Today, I approach each new day with a sense of anticipation. I wonder, *Who am I gonna meet today? What can I do to make someone else's life better? Where will the next opportunity present itself?* To me, this is the secret to happiness. I may never discover the meaning of life, but being generous is what makes my life meaningful!"

Pete and Mico sat in silence for a good long while, each in their own thoughts.

Mico finally broke the silence, "Something else I discovered: The universe is not a cruel place for taking away my Jewell; everything dies—even dragons die, I think. Well, I'm not so sure about that one, but my point is, I acknowledge that life is hard and then you die. But, if you know how and where to look, there is beauty and treasures to be found."

"Thank you Mico. I mean that from the bottom of my heart."

"You're welcome, son," Mico said as he clasped Pete's forearm and smiled contentedly.

"So, in the end, how did you get rescued?" Pete asked. "I mean you're here, right, so a ship must have come by and picked you up or something?"

"The way I see it, I was rescued the night Lóng pulled me from a watery grave," Mico corrected.

"Oh, of course, right," Pete replied. "I guess what I mean is, how is it that we are sitting here today?"

"Well, one morning Lóng asked me a curious question."

"If you had a choice to go back to where you are from or start over somewhere new, which would you choose?"

"I'd go back," Mico said, without hesitation.

"It's a big wonderful world out there," Lóng countered, "with lots of adventure to be found. Are you sure you'd want to go back?"

"When Jewell died, I lost my most precious jewel, literally. I lost

my reason for being, but these past few months I have learned two important things, and I've made one amazing, new friend."

The dragon raised an eyebrow inquisitively, "What are those two things, my friend?"

"Number one: What we have once enjoyed and deeply loved we can never lose, for all that we love deeply becomes a part of us."

"Quite right," Lóng said, "and what about the other?"

"Be generous."

The dragon smiled. "You have discovered my secret treasure, Mico, and the most amazing thing is that the more you give away, the more you shall receive."

"At that, we both laughed, long and hard," Mico said. "We danced on the deck like sailors and embraced until that dragon almost squeezed the breath right out of me!

"And at that very moment," Mico said, "I heard a ship's horn blast twice. I looked up and there she was on my starboard side—a big beautiful cargo ship—heading straight for me. I ran to the cabin to grab my flare gun, and when I came back, Lóng was nowhere in sight … just disappeared.

"I shot off the flare with a mix of emotions that would be impossible to explain," Mico sighed.

"The odd thing," he continued, "was when they brought me on board, the crew insisted that only a day had passed since that fierce storm!"

"That's strange," Pete replied, "I thought you said you were out there for nearly four and a half months. How do you explain that?"

"Well, I've thought about this many times," Mico said. "You see, dragons are magical beasts. They have the power to appear and disappear, and they control rivers and lakes, storms and water in all its forms. It's not that much of a stretch to conclude that they have the ability to control time as well."

"That seems logical to me," Pete said. "So, wait a minute, did you ever see Lóng again?"

"Why don't you stop by my boat tomorrow," Mico said with a twinkle in his eye, "and find that out for yourself?"

Thomas John Dennis

PEGGY'S DREAM

She stepped up to the front door of the rectory, took a deep breath, and rang the bell.

xAfter a few moments, when nobody answered, she rang the bell again. Still no answer. She breathed a sigh of relief, turned, and started walking back to her car.

Just then, the pastor, Father George Walsh, opened the door and shouted after her, "Hello!" Craning his neck, he called out, "Mary Margaret? Is that you? I don't think I've seen you since the funeral."

"Crap," she said under her breath and turned around. "Hello, Father George, I was wondering if you could hear my confession?" She looked down, embarrassed. *This was a stupid idea*, she thought.

"Oh ... well, I'm kind of in the middle of something," he said wiping his hands on a dish towel. "Are you sure this can't wait until Saturday afternoon? I usually hear confessions on Saturday from one to two."

"I'm sorry," she said. "I know I should have made an appointment or something. I can come back another time." She turned to go, and then added as a sort of explanation, "It's just, well, my friend Mico suggested it might be good for me ..."

Father George's ears perked up, "Oh, did Mico send you here?" Then, without waiting for a reply he continued, "Why didn't you say so? Come on in." He opened the door wide. Closing the door behind her, he said, "Whenever Mico sends someone to me, I know they mean business. Why don't you take a seat in the parlor over here to the right. I'll just be a minute. I need to take something out of the oven, and I'll be right back." Then he disappeared down the hall.

Whatever he was baking, it sure smelled good. She didn't take a seat; she was too nervous. The parlor looked like she had imagined. *The furniture is a bit dated*, she thought, *but it looks comfortable enough*. The only artwork was a reproduction of an old painting of St. George slaying the dragon on one wall and a crucifix on the other. Under the painting there was a blue and white Chinese vase with a dried flower arrangement in it.

She looked closer at the vase. There were dragons on it as well. "Oh my gosh, dragons seem to be popping up everywhere these days," she said softly to herself.

"What was that about dragons?" Father George asked as he entered the room.

"Oh, did I say that out loud? I didn't mean to. It was nothing," she added, brushing away the thought.

"Come sit down," Father George encouraged her. Then he set two glasses of water down on the coffee table and sat down in one of the chairs. "Would you be interested in staying for dinner? Veggie chili and cornbread. I made it myself—from scratch."

"I don't remember the last time someone prepared a homemade meal for me," she said wistfully. "I usually just eat at the diner. It smells so good, but I can't. Thanks anyway."

"Okay then, shall we get started?" Father George took one of those little purple ribbon-like stoles out of his pocket and put it around his neck.

"Uhh … aren't we supposed to do this in the confessional?"

"Not unless you really want to. I mean, I guess if you want to sit behind a screen in that little dark closet we can, but it's not like I don't already know who you are."

"You've got a point there," she replied, and surrendered by sitting down into the chair opposite the priest. "Let's get this over with."

Father George got an amused look on his face.

"Oh my gosh, did I say that out loud too?" she asked, mortified.

He smiled and nodded.

"I'm sorry, it's just, well, I haven't done this in a while."

"So how long has it been since your last confession?"

"Well," she thought for a moment, "I probably haven't been since confirmation in the eighth grade," she said sheepishly.

"Looks like this is going to take a while," Father George said with a broad smile and a wink.

"Father!" She shot back with mock indignation.

"Oh, I'm sorry, Mary Margaret, just trying to loosen you up a bit. Relax, for goodness' sake. This is not the Inquisition—it's supposed to be an encounter with God's mercy."

"For clarity's sake, Father, nobody's ever called me Mary Margaret except my mother. At the diner, people just call me Peggy or Peg."

"My apologies again Mary—err, I mean—Peggy. I'm sure I knew that, it's just your mother used to talk about you all the time. It was, 'Mary Margaret this …' and 'Mary Margaret that.' She was so proud of you, you know."

"That's kind of why I'm here, Father," she said. "And you don't have to apologize, it's actually nice hearing someone call me that again. Oh, I almost forgot—thank you for the card you sent me on her birthday. That was so thoughtful. Nobody else remembered, or at least acknowledged it was her birthday."

"You're welcome, I know birthdays and anniversaries can be hard. How long has it been since she died? About eight, nine months perhaps?"

"Yeah, as a matter of fact, it's nine months tomorrow. I thought I'd be over this by now, I mean, she was sick for a long time, it's not like I didn't know it was coming," Peggy replied. "I was doing fine at first. I put on a happy face." Then, adding in a confidential tone, "The customers tip more when you smile.

"Besides, there wasn't a lot to do, I was already doing all her financial stuff anyway, and we pretty much cleaned out the house when she went into the nursing home. Most of her personal things were put in storage. I still have to go through it. I just haven't been able to do that yet. I don't know why, I mean, I'm a strong woman—I got that from her. Raising two kids all by herself after Dad died, it wasn't easy. But God, she was always so positive, I don't know how she did it."

"Like mother, like daughter. It seems you managed to pull it off yourself after the divorce, happy face and all."

Peggy was at first surprised. *How could he know about the divorce?* she wondered, but then she realized her mother would have held nothing back from Father George. "That was different," Peggy said. "I had her to help me. She was always there in the background cheering me on. Somehow she always knew just what to say. Because I work the night shift, she was also my built-in babysitter. I couldn't fail, I didn't want to disappoint her."

"Now wait a minute, you could have never disappointed her, even if you'd have robbed a bank."

A huge lump rose in Peggy's throat as she tried to choke back the tears.

"You're allowed to cry, Mary Margaret," Father George said, using her proper name intentionally. "Your mother was one of the kindest people I've known. I'd petition Rome for canonization except for the fact that she cursed like a sailor."

Peggy laughed at that and wiped away a tear.

"Look, your mother was in your life from the first moment of your conception. I think you're allowed to grieve for as long as you need. Besides, it's going to take a while to figure out how to navigate in the world without her."

"How long is that gonna take?" Peggy pleaded.

"A lot longer than nine months, let me tell you."

"Shit," Peggy said before catching herself. "Sorry about that."

"That's okay, we'll add swearing to your long list of sins." The priest grinned. "Besides, we know where you got your potty mouth, don't we?"

"Father," Peggy said, "I let her down." She started crying, the tears rolled down her face.

Father George paused before he handed her some tissues; he had learned that offering a tissue too soon often shuts people down, and he didn't want to give Peggy the wrong message.

After regaining some composure, Peggy went on, "I should have been there. When she died, I should have been there!"

Father George nodded, encouraging her to keep talking.

"You know, before she went into the nursing home, and then after, when my shift was over, I always stopped by and had breakfast with her. It was our routine, and I know she loved it as much as I did." Peggy wiped her nose, then continued, "That morning, Bud asked me if I could take an extra shift—one of the waitresses' little one was sick again and I was going to call Mom to tell her I'd stop by later, but the diner was so busy that I forgot. And then, they couldn't get ahold of me so they called Mico, who, by some kind of divine intervention, just happened to be there at the time … and, Father, it was like slow motion or something. I saw him from across the room answer his phone, and then he looked over at me, and I knew, I knew that instant that she was gone."

Peggy buried her face in her hands and wept.

Father George sat quietly, a model of compassion. He silently offered a prayer of thanksgiving that the dam she'd built up inside had finally broken. He also gave thanks for the gift of being invited into the grace of this moment.

"Father, I didn't get to say goodbye. I didn't get to tell her how much I loved her. And most of all, I think about how she died alone and afraid, and I wasn't there to hold her hand."

"Peggy," Father George said as softly and as authoritatively as he could, "of all the people I have known, I can guarantee you that your mother was not afraid of dying. You know as well as I that prayer she prayed every day, 'I cannot see very far ahead, but when I come to where the horizon closes down, a new prospect will open before me, and I shall meet it with peace.' We printed it on her mass card, remember? And just for the record, I would like to believe that she wasn't alone in the end, that there was someone to greet her and escort her to the other side. You know what I'm talking about?"

Peggy nodded.

"Look, I know you feel bad about the timing of it all,

that you didn't get to say goodbye, but it's not up to us. Just because you feel guilty about something doesn't mean it was a sin. Is that what you feel you need to confess? Are you thinking you broke the fifth commandment or something because it just so happened on the day the Lord called her home, you chose to do a kind act for a coworker instead of having breakfast with your mother?" The priest paused long enough to see if what he was saying was sinking in; however, he was on a roll and he wasn't about to stop there.

"And another thing, she knows how much you love her. I'm sorry you didn't get the chance to say it one last time, but let me ask this: How close to the time of death does it have to be in order to count? Over the course of your relationship, you must have said those words a hundred million times. And as long as we're counting, how many times did you express it without words but in your actions?" He paused, not expecting an answer. "You see where I'm going here? She knows, my dear, she knows."

Peggy nodded again. They sat in silence for a long while.

Then Peggy spoke up, "I want to believe all that Father, I really do, but I keep having the same bad dream, over and over. In my dream, I'm racing down the hall of the nursing home to her room to tell her goodbye and that I love her, but when I get to her door a dragon appears out of nowhere and I can't get in. Every time I just scream, and then I wake up."

"Hmm," Father George said scratching his chin. "Just out of curiosity, what color was the dragon?"

"What's that got to do with anything?" Peggy asked a little confused and annoyed.

"Just humor me, what color was the dragon?"

"Blue, green maybe, I don't know, it was kind of iridescent, maybe both. I distinctly remember it had a mane almost like a lion and really sharp teeth. Oh, and it also had horns like the devil himself."

"Did the dragon have wings?"

"No, as a matter of fact, it was more like the dragons

you see all over Chinatown. Why are you asking?"

"Well," pointing over his shoulder at the painting of St. George, "you can't grow up Catholic with the name George and not have a curiosity about dragons. When I was a kid I even had an imaginary friend who was a dragon, but that's a story for another day. Anyway, I've learned a thing or two over the years, and I find it curious that in your dream you encountered a Chinese water dragon."

"Why is that curious?" she asked.

"Because in Chinese mythology that particular dragon has dominion over rivers, lakes, the sea, thunderstorms, and water in all its forms."

Peggy looked at him blankly. "I'm not sure what that has to do with me?"

"Of course. I'm sorry, I just think it's interesting that a water dragon appeared in your dream because if this dragon has power over water in all its forms, it's got to have power over those 'waves' of grief too. You see my point?"

Peggy nodded, but she was still not sure if she was buying into what he was saying.

"Did the dragon say anything?"

"No, every time I have the dream, I wake up at that point."

"Look," Father George said, "I'm not an expert on dreams, but I do know that there is more than one place in the Bible where an important message was communicated through a dream. Think of St. Joseph's dream and the Holy Family's flight into Egypt.

"If you have the dream again," he suggested, "you might want to ask the dragon why it's come to you or what it wants." Then as an afterthought, he said, "Oh, yeah, you might want to bow first—it is a Chinese dragon after all."

"Doesn't the Bible associate dragons with the devil?"

"Yes, it does," Father George said. "In particular, in the book of Revelation, dragons are associated with chaos and destruction, and the struggle between good and evil. But what you've got to understand is that the book of Revelation is apocalyptic literature. It's about the end time, and it's full of symbolic language, some of which I'm not sure if even scripture scholars have a clear understanding of what it originally meant to the early Christian community. There are other references to dragons too—for example, one of the Psalms, and Job, and the book of Isaiah mention a sea monster called Leviathan, which could be interpreted as some kind of water dragon."

Father George shifted in his chair and continued, "However, in Chinese mythology, we see a whole other perspective. In most Eastern traditions, dragons are associated with the positive and creative side of chaos. They are also symbols of strength and power. To be associated with them brings good fortune and good luck.

"I think of dragons as messengers, kind of like angels, born in the primordial soup at the beginning of time. They have the power to bring order or chaos, they can travel between this world and the next. I don't think they represent the devil so much as they've come to symbolize everything that scares us, especially death. So, once more, if you have the dream again, ask the dragon what it wants—its answer just might surprise you."

"Okay," Peggy replied, "but if you get a call one of these days that I've died from a heart attack in my sleep, you'll know why!"

"If that happens, I'm sure it will have more to do with all those burgers and fries you've had at that diner," Father George joked. "Maybe that's why you're here. You've come to confess your complicity in the heart attacks of customers, past, present, and future?"

"Oh, Father," Peggy said as she dismissed his dig with a wave of her hand, "save your preaching for the choir."

They both laughed at that. "Touché," Father George said, "touché."

"So, I don't need to confess that I failed my mother?"

"No," the priest said reassuringly, "but, I'm wondering if there are any other burdens you've been carrying for the past *thirty years* that you feel it's time to give to God?"

"Ahh, well, there might be a few things, in addition to not going to mass, that I should probably mention ..." And she did. Peggy released the guilt and shame she carried for so many years, and when the priest laid his hands on her head and prayed the words of absolution, it felt like a terrible weight had been lifted from her shoulders.

"If I knew it was going to feel this good to confess my sins, I would have done it years ago!"

"I know, right? That's what I keep trying to tell people! ... So, you sure you're not interested in some of that homemade veggie chili and cornbread?"

"Well," Peggy confessed, "It might be kind of nice to have someone wait on me for a change."

"Okay then," Father George said happily. "Be careful, though, I just might convert you into a vegetarian."

"Oh, I doubt that Father, but, you never know ..."

A few days later

As Father George was getting ready to head over to the church for weekday mass, the phone rang.

"Good morning, Father Walsh speaking. May I help you?"

"Oh Father, you sound so formal over the phone! I'm so glad I caught you before mass. This is Peggy. Do you have a minute?"

"I sure do. What's up?" He could hear the excitement in her voice.

"Well, I talked to the dragon! In my dream, I mean, and you will never guess what it said to me." She didn't pause long enough for him to respond.

"Same as before, I'm racing down the hall to my mother's room and I get to her door and the dragon appears, only this time, I do what you suggested, I bow and ask the dragon, 'What do you want?' and you will never guess what it said!"

"I can't even begin to guess. What did it say?"

"'Well, it's about time!' the dragon said. Can you believe it?" Peggy laughed. "Then it said, 'Are you going to wake up on me again? Because if you do that again, I'm afraid I'm going to have to take more drastic measures.' I was not at all interested in finding out what those might be."

"So, then I bowed again for good measure, and mustering all the courage I could find, I said, 'No, dragon, I'm not leaving until you tell me what you want, and why you are keeping me from seeing my mother.'"

———

"First of all," the dragon said rather formally, "we have not been properly introduced. You are Mary Margaret, firstborn of my good friend Catherine. You may address me as Lóng," the dragon added with a bow.

"Secondly," Lóng continued, "you are mistaken. It is not I who have kept you from seeing your mother. I have been trying to get your attention for weeks!"

"I'm sorry, I didn't understand," Peggy replied.

"I must say, this is something that I rarely have to deal with. Your mother," Lóng said sighing, "she is one of the most obstinate people I have ever met. She has shut her door and refuses to move on!"

"Move on, to where?"

"Beyond the horizon, of course. She refuses to leave until she gets the chance to tell you goodbye. Would you please go talk to her so we can continue her journey?"

Peggy stepped gingerly past the dragon and knocked on the door, "Mom? It's Mary Margaret, are you okay?"

The door opened wide and there stood her mother. She was radiant, dressed in her Sunday best. She was also wearing ruby slippers, like the kind Dorothy wore in The Wizard of Oz.

"Oh, my dear, I'm so sorry." Catherine threw her arms around her daughter, and they hugged for what seemed like an eternity.

Loosening her embrace and looking into her daughter's eyes, she said, "I'm so proud of you! I love you so much! I am so sorry that I died without giving you the chance to say goodbye, the timing of it all wasn't up to me." She looked over Peggy's shoulder at Lóng scornfully.

The dragon huffed, "And people think I'm stubborn!"

"I couldn't leave without giving you a gift—here, let me put it on

you."

———————

"Then, out of nowhere she pulls out this ratty, old mink stole my father gave her before he died. God, she loved that thing!" Peggy added.

"What happened next?" Father George asked.

"She wrapped it around my shoulders and said, 'It's up to you now, Mary Margaret.'" Peggy paused for a moment as her voice cracked.

"Then she took my face in her hands and touched her forehead to mine and said again, 'I'm so proud of you.'"

It was Father George's turn to choke back some tears.

Peggy finished her story, "Then she placed her hand on the dragon's tail, clicked her heels three times, and they both kind of floated down the hall toward this bright light. The whole time she was looking back, blowing kisses and mouthing the words, 'I love you,' until they faded from view."

"Wow! What an exit."

"That was my mother, always a flair for the dramatic."

"So, what do you think?" the priest asked, proud of himself for his skillful use of open-ended questions.

"What do I think? I think I'm gonna go get that ratty, old mink stole out of storage and have it sewn onto a coat that will fit me."

They both laughed heartily.

"Well, listen, I'm afraid I've got to cut this short," Father George said checking his watch.

"Oh, right, you've probably got mass and all."

"Right. So, I'll see you at mass on Sunday, then?"

"I'll be the one in the ratty, old mink stole," she smiled through the phone. "I can't thank you enough, Father. You really helped me, more than you will ever know."

"You're welcome, Peggy, but you might also want to thank God, or your lucky stars—or Lóng for that matter, the next time you meet, if there is a next time. After all, it's not every person who gets to meet a dragon."

PETE'S WILD RIDE

Pete shut the front door behind him and locked it. He no longer felt the urge to call out his wife's name every time he came home, but stepping across that threshold continued to serve as a pointed reminder, two-plus years after her death, that he was still very much alone. Having been out to dinner that evening with old friends, the yearning for his wife was especially great. "God, if they would just stop trying to fix me up with every widow and divorcée they know, I'd be fine," he said to the four walls. He hardly even noticed when he was talking out loud anymore; he'd been doing it for so long. He changed into a T-shirt and shorts, and then poured a glass of wine and sat down—plopped really—into his leather recliner.

His friends meant well, he knew that but, "If they had just given me a day's warning instead of springing her on me at the last minute, I could have prepared myself," he said. Instead of a relaxing evening out with friends, Pete had felt blindsided, defensive, and as awkward as a teenager on a first date.

"It's not like I haven't put on a few pounds myself," he said, "but come on, really?" In reality, the friend of a friend to whom he was introduced appeared healthy and active enough for a woman of their age. She was actually quite nice, but Pete couldn't stop himself from comparing every woman he met to his wife. Of course none of them measured up, in one respect or another. To top it off, across the room at the restaurant, he saw an old couple holding hands; that did him in.

"It's just not fair," he mumbled. He could feel his mood continuing to spiral downward, and he knew better than to let it go there, but tonight felt like an exception given the evening. A storm was coming, and he was more than willing to let the darkness envelop him. "We had a plan," he lamented over and over. "What's the point now?" was a question he'd asked himself a thousand times. Also, there were the many other versions of that question: "Why bother?" Or, simply the sarcastic comment, "Yeah, I'm sure that's going to be fun." "And, if one more person says the words *new* and *normal* in the same sentence, I'm going to lose it," he warned, shaking his fist in the air. "New normal, I hate that phrase."

Just then, a clap of thunder sounded as if in reply. Pete was actually startled. Then he laughed at himself. He was reminded of the first time he met Mico. "That crazy old coot." For a moment, Pete had actually bought into the fisherman's yarn. "Dragons," he said, shaking his head. Mico had, in fact, become a good friend and mentor, even if the old fella was a bit eccentric at times.

The night they met, Pete found himself in an all-night diner down by the marina. He knew he'd had a few too many, and he wanted to sober up a little before driving home. Then Mico hobbled in and sat down on the stool next to him. They had got to talking, and in the midst of it all, Mico shared his dragon tale. "I was such a sucker," Pete said, though once he even went so far as to take Mico up on his offer to meet the dragon. But, of course, Pete shouted aloud, "There is no such thing as dragons."

Another clap of thunder seemed to answer angrily. Pete gulped the last of his wine, and just as he got up to refill his glass, the lights went out.

"Damn!" Pete cursed as he stubbed his toe on the leg of the coffee table. "Where did I put that flashlight?" He searched all of the obvious places that were accessible in the dark. Then he remembered his wife was always the one to prepare for such emergencies. "Great," he mumbled. "Another thing I need to put on my list of things to do: buy a flashlight," he complained. Pete eventually ended up lighting a few candles and starting a fire in the fireplace before settling back in his chair with a refill of wine. "How romantic," he said. "Cheers." These evenings of drinking and talking to himself were becoming increasingly common.

A storm of this intensity had not been anticipated. "The forecast called for light showers," Pete grumbled, but this one was way worse than that—thunder and lightning, driving rain, and gale-force winds. "It would be just my luck if a tree fell on the house," Pete whined. "Go ahead," he yelled at the storm, "give me all you got!" Right on cue, the front door flew open with a bang. The wind howled as Pete leaped out of his chair and ran to the opened door. He slipped on the now rain-slick surface tiles, fell, and banged his head on the floor. Scrambling to his feet, he teetered like a drunk, but was eventually able to secure the door.

"That was weird," Pete said rubbing the back of his head. "I'm sure I locked that when I came home." He stepped gingerly, so as to not slip again. The candles had been blown out, but the fireplace continued to burn eerily bright. It felt like the barometric pressure had suddenly changed, and the hairs on the back of his neck stood on end as an inexplicable feeling washed like a wave over his body. A low, almost imperceptible rumble—kind of like the sound whales make to communicate across vast distances of ocean—filled the house and reverberated inside his chest.

"So, there's no such thing as dragons?" said a deep, menacing voice.

Pete looked around but saw nothing. "I must be losing it," he said, shaking his head.

"I'll say!" came the voice in quick reply. It seemed to be coming from a dark corner of the room.

"Who's there?" Pete exclaimed, "I demand to know!"

"Oh, you know very well who it is," Lóng said, while slowly drifting into the glow of the fire. The dragon's long, snake-like body and tail meandered like a river as its immenseness filled the room.

"Holy shit!" Pete said, stumbling backward, his eyes fixed on the levitating dragon. Flattening himself against the wall, he slowly inched his way back toward the front door.

"Have you thought through this exit strategy?" the dragon inquired. "Where exactly do you think you're going to go?"

Pete stopped, thought it over, and visibly slumped like a condemned man surrendering to his fate.

"Lóng?" Pete asked in disbelief.

The dragon nodded. "I believe you owe me an apology."

"An apology? I don't understand. An apology for …?"

"For doubting my existence."

"I … I thought you were a metaphor," Pete offered.

"Would that make me any less real? Just because you have not yet seen someone, does not mean they do not exist. Take God for instance."

"I don't believe in God," Pete said flatly.

"My point exactly."

"What I refuse to believe in, is a God who would let children suffer," Pete spat out as if he were responding to a schoolyard taunt.

"What you mean to say," Lóng said in a slow, measured, grown-up tone of voice, "is that you refuse to believe in a God who would allow your wife to die from cancer."

"Yeah, you're right! And the Holocaust, and famine, and pestilence, and poverty and injustice—all of it, across the ages! You name it!" Pete seemed finished, but then added, "And climate change! All-powerful, my ass!"

"Don't try that redirecting trick on me," Lóng said quietly, "I wasn't born yesterday, you know. I have literally seen it all. I may have even, indirectly, been responsible for some of that destruction and chaos myself.

"You are aggrieved that your mate has died, and that is a sadness that cuts to the heart, but you are left with a fundamental choice: you can either allow that wound to fester, in which case, I will leave you to your own demise, or you can see that wound as an opening to the suffering of others and respond accordingly."

Pete covered his face with his hands and slid to the floor. "But it's not fair—we were supposed to grow old together, we had a 401(k), we had a plan." Pete wept bitterly. "It's just not fair."

"Who told you life is fair? It's *not* fair. Life is anything but fair. It is not fair that by the circumstance of birth, some are born into poverty and others into wealth. It is not fair that the rich and powerful benefit at the expense of others and that justice is seldom measured out evenly. It is not fair that tornadoes rip through communities, splintering some houses while leaving others untouched.

"Look at your own life through the eyes of someone else and you will see just how unfair life can be. You live in this country, how fair is that? You have a good job, and a 401(k) and an education, how fair is that? You have friends to support you, how fair is that? You have your health, how fair is that? And you have gorged yourself on the sweet nectar of love. How fair is that?"

Lóng could see his argument was not having its intended effect. "Let me put it another way. You think, somehow, that you have been cheated because your life hasn't turned out as planned?"

"Yes!" Pete spat back. "Yes, we were cheated! If the doctors had caught it sooner she might still be alive. If we had been told that there were new drug trials we could try, or [and this being his real grievance] if I had insisted she see her doctor instead of dismissing her complaints as hypochondria, we might at least have had more time."

"More time? Perhaps. However, you are not considering how much extra time she got because of the care she received from you and the medical professionals. Nor are you considering how more time might have meant more pain and suffering.

"While you are at it, you might also want to consider how much time you have wasted ruminating over what might have been, instead of engaging with the moment at hand."

At some level, what Lóng was saying was starting to sink in, but Pete wasn't ready to hear it all yet. He continued with his protests, "But she was such a good person," and, shaking his head, "She didn't deserve it."

"Yes, she was fundamentally a good person. You were blessed to have had her in your life. You are, no doubt, a better person because of her. And so are you—a good person, I mean. But, I need to tell you," Lóng cautioned, "all this negativity, the storms you are building up inside you, are driving people away."

Dragons can get away with saying certain hard truths, and this particular truth Lóng had spoken was clearly an arrow that found its mark. Pete said, "I know that's true. I don't even like me right now. I just wish I could see what my life will be like in the future. Will I ever find love again? Will I be happy again? I used to be happy, and grateful to be alive. I just wish you had a crystal ball or something so that I could know if, in the end, it was worth it."

"You are in luck," said the dragon. "That is one wish that is within my power to grant." Then, swinging its tail around and cracking it like a whip, the dragon commanded, "Grab ahold and hang on tight. This is going to be a wild ride."

Despite being locked, the door swung open again. Lóng, with Pete in tow, flew out the door and up, up into the stormy night sky. The dragon opened its mouth and lightning emanated from it with a blinding flash. The deafening sound of thunder followed. This happened again and again. Pete lost all sense of space and time, he just held on with all his might. He closed his eyes, thinking that would help; it didn't. The dragon began to fly in circles, slowly at first, but then with increasing speed, creating a vortex like a tornado. Pete could hold on no longer. He lost his grip and flew into the darkness. "Nooooo!" he cried.

Falling at first, and then sensing he was slowly floating downward, Pete relaxed. He landed like a feather in an unfamiliar place.

Lóng drifted down next to him. "Where am I?" Pete asked the dragon.

"You wanted to see your future. This is one possibility. Lóng pointed with a clawed hand at a gray, institutional-looking building with plastic bushes in pots on either side of the door. "Go inside," Lóng commanded.

Pete did as he was told. It was a nursing home, and by the looks of things, not a very good one. The stench of incontinence was so overwhelming Pete had to breathe through his mouth. He walked past a line of old people in wheelchairs parked along the wall; some asleep, others seemingly following him with their eyes. The staff scurried about, apparently oblivious to the residents and Pete, not to mention the dragon. Lóng appeared beside him, the dragon's long body stretching back down the hallway. Lóng pointed at a door and said, "Enter."

Pete looked at Lóng, then at the door, then back at Lóng. "What's in there?" Pete asked tentatively.

"Your future."

Pete pushed the door, and it opened to a large ward with about six beds, all separated by ceiling-to-floor curtains. The blue light from fluorescent bulbs was uncomfortable to Pete's eyes; he wondered if it bothered the residents. He peeked around a curtain. It was an old man with a distended belly and one leg amputated. Behind the next, another old man, this one contracted into a fetal position. He was little more than skin and bones, his mouth gaping open, his eyes closed.

Somehow Pete knew what lay behind curtain number three. He hesitated; the dragon nudged him forward with the tip of its snout. "Look at what we came to see."

Pete was compelled to look, and there in the bed he lay staring out blankly into the room. His hair appeared as if it hadn't been washed in weeks. Pete in the bed was thinner than the one he saw in the mirror every day, but it was clearly his own face. The most disturbing thing was that the Pete in the bed didn't appear to be too many years older than the Pete standing next to it.

One of the other men in the ward called out for someone to help him. The Pete in the bed yelled at him, "Shut the hell up!" The Pete who was standing by the bed attempted to intervene.

"Don't bother," Lóng said, "the staff can't see you or hear you."

"But what about the people in the hall?"

"They have dementia. The veil is thinner for them. At this stage, they are closer to the next world than to this one. They are simply awaiting my return."

"I don't understand," Pete said.

"Of course, you don't," Lóng replied. "Let me put it another way, the ones in the hall can see ghosts."

"But I'm not a ghost," Pete declared.

"To them you are," said the dragon.

Turning his attention back to the Pete in the bed, he asked Lóng, "What's wrong with him—err—me? Why am I here?"

"There is nobody to care for you."

"I don't understand. What about my son and daughter?"

"You and your son are no longer on speaking terms; you rejected him when he told you he was in love with another man. Your daughter comes to visit on occasion but only out of a sense of obligation. When she comes, you usually curse at her for leaving you here."

"Can you blame me?" Pete protested in his own defense. "Just look at this place."

"This is where they put the old and the indigent in your country. It is not a nice place, but it is better than the alley they found you in."

"What do you mean? I have a house, I have friends …"

"*Had*," Lóng said. "Past tense."

Pete was having trouble taking it all in. He just kept repeating, "I don't understand … I don't understand …"

Lóng let him piece together the story in his own mind before replying. Then he filled in a few of the details Pete needed in order to understand. "After your wife died, you started drinking—a lot. That night in the diner, the night you met Mico, you told him to get lost. You drove him away, just like you did all your friends. So, of course, he wasn't there to encourage you to talk to your old boss."

Pete picked up the story there, "So I stayed at that start-up long enough to get fired, I'm guessing—that miserable little snot …"

"Careful," Lóng intervened, "you deserved it. That young entrepreneur might have given you more of a chance, but it would not have made much of a difference. The outcome would have been the same. You made some attempts at looking for another job, but who would want to hire a man with a drinking problem, and so close to retirement age?

"You started out on this trajectory, and although there were several points where your story might have been turned around, you stayed stuck repeating the same refrain, 'It isn't fair.' 'We had a plan.' 'What's the point?'

"You gave up on life, Peter," the dragon said, using his proper name. "In many ways, you are worse than those people down the hall."

Pete was quiet. He looked down at the Pete in the bed. "How old am I? What's wrong with me?" he asked Lóng.

"Does it matter? The man in that bed died inside a long time ago."

They stood in silence for a long while.

"There is one more place I want you to see. Take hold of my tail."

Pete did as he was told. Lóng turned and quickly exited the room. Pete held on tight and was dragged behind him. Again, the dragon flew up into the night sky, only this time there was no storm. Again, the dragon flew in circles, increasing its speed until Pete could hold on no longer. Trusting Lóng this time, he let go and drifted back down to solid ground. They were back at Pete's house; the lights were on in the living room, casting a warm glow on the trees outside.

"I don't understand," Pete said.

"You will when you go inside."

Pete did as he was told. He approached the front door and he could hear music and laughter coming from inside. His heart was filled with gladness. He opened the door and called out his wife's name. But there was no answer, of course.

"There are certain things I cannot do, and one of them is to bring back the dead." Lóng nudged him, "Go on ..."

Pete stepped into the living room and saw himself lying in a hospital bed next to the fireplace. He was propped up on pillows, smiling. Right next to the bed, Peggy, the waitress from the diner, was sitting looking lovingly into his eyes. His son and daughter were at his bedside too. On the couch, his son-in-law and another man he did not recognize were entertaining his grandkids. There were a couple other people in the room too, that he guessed were Peggy's children—they certainly looked like her.

On the fireplace mantel, there were about a dozen pictures, including one of his wife and one of Mico. There was a wedding photo of him and Peggy, as well as pictures of other family members, past and present.

Pete eagerly looked at Lóng.

"Ask your questions," Lóng said.

"I don't have any questions," Pete replied. "It's all pretty clear to me." He looked around the room contentedly. "Well, I guess I have just one: which of these two futures is the real one?"

"That is up to you, my friend."

"You mean I can choose?" Pete asked. "If I can choose, I definitely want this one." Then adding, "Although, admittedly, I would have wanted to live longer."

"Life," Lóng said, "has always been about quality, not quantity. The two scenes I have shown you tonight are only two prospects among an infinite number of possible futures. Every choice, every decision you make, from getting up in the morning to crossing the street, can lead to a different ending."

"Then how will I know what to do?"

"You won't. You are just going to have to trust your inner dragon."

"How do I do that?"

"Don't overthink it," Lóng replied. "Just focus on the moment at hand and live intentionally, authentically, gratefully, expectantly."

"I think I understand. Can we go back now, to the time that was before all this?"

"Why don't you ride up front this time? Climb aboard." Lóng bowed low, and Pete did as he was told. He grabbed hold of the dragon's mane, wrapped his legs tightly around Lóng's neck, and off they went.

Lóng said, "Let's take the scenic route," and instead of going in circles, this time they headed due west and ended up out over the ocean.

Pete had flown before, but that was in an airplane at thirty thousand feet. Below him was a vast expanse of ocean, as far as he could see. The waves shimmered like silver in the moonlight. Above him, stars—more stars than he could ever imagine. Was he scared? To be honest, a little bit, but he reminded himself he was in the company of a dragon. He had never experienced such a thrill in his entire life; for the first time in a long while he felt alive! It was exhilarating. Pete felt a deep sense of abiding peace. *It's going to be all right*, Pete said to himself, *it's going to be okay*.

Lóng made a wide arc in the sky and headed back toward the coast. They arrived at the marina just as the sun was coming up. There were fishermen preparing for the day's catch, but nobody seemed to notice the little man atop a huge dragon flying overhead. Lóng dropped Pete off at a deserted spot on the beach nearby.

"Before I forget—I'm really sorry."

"For what?" Lóng asked.

"That I doubted you."

"Oh, for that," Lóng remembered his initial introduction. "Don't worry about it. I get that all the time."

"No, I'm serious. I've come to realize that I need to believe in you. I need to believe that there are powers greater than myself, that there is something that can bring order to chaos, something that can help me calm the storms of grief."

Lóng quoted scripture, "Blessed are the eyes that have not seen and yet believe."

"What's that?" Pete asked.

"Oh, nothing," the dragon replied. "Listen, since you brought up the subject of forgetting, I need to tell you something that might make you a little upset."

Pete looked at Lóng open-eyed.

"So, the thing is, you are not going to remember any

of this …"

"What? Wait, I don't understand." Pete said.

"Yeah, see, I can't go around letting people know when they are going to die. It upsets the balance of nature. I am sorry."

"So, you mean I'm not going to remember that any of this happened?" Pete felt betrayed; he felt the euphoria he had been experiencing begin to quickly slip away. "Then why show me in the first place? I could easily fall back into that dark place and head down the path that leads to isolation, and I don't want to end up there."

"No, of course not," Lóng said. "What I want you to know is that I believe in you too. I was given the ability to see into the heart, and when I look into yours, I see the heart of a dragon. I see a strength and beauty that you cannot see—right now, that is. Why do you think I have invested so much energy in you? All you need, is to believe in *you* too."

"So then, how do I hold on to this experience?"

"Pete, I want you to close your eyes."

Pete did as he was told.

Lóng said, "You may not remember with your mind this night or the events that I have shown you, but whereas the mind forgets, the heart remembers. Look within and remember the feeling you had in your living room. See the people who are gathered there and find the place in your heart that corresponds to each of them. Feel the warmth and peace of that moment; feel the admiration, the love that binds, and yes, even the inevitable grief that comes from separation."

Lóng paused long enough for Pete to anchor the feeling. "Now, remember the feeling you had with me out there under the stars."

Again, Lóng paused.

When Pete had engaged with these feelings, Lóng reached out and touched Pete's chest and …

Pete awoke on the beach a little dazed, a little confused, but with no anxiety as to how he got there or why. He simply sat on the beach for a while and felt the abiding peace of the place. "Why don't I come down here more often?" he said to himself.

Later he realized he had another feeling; it was hunger. Knowing that Bud's Diner was just a short walk away, he got up and headed in that direction.

Upon entering, Peggy greeted him warmly, "Hey, sweetie, what a nice surprise to see you at this time of the day. I'm afraid Mico isn't here. He was here late last night, so I don't think we'll be seeing him again anytime soon."

"That's okay, Peggy, I didn't come in to see him, I came to see you."

Pete's reply surprised both of them.

"Oh really?" Peggy felt a little flutter inside.

"Yeah, don't you get off right about now?"

Peggy nodded.

"Good, I was wondering if you'd be interested in me making you breakfast?" Pete said tentatively. He had no idea where he got the idea or the courage to ask her out, but he decided to trust his heart and go with it.

She paused for a second, unsure what to say.

"Oh, I'm sorry," Pete said, back peddling, "maybe there is a rule about dating the customers or something?"

"No, no, there's no rule about that." She paused for just a second and then said, "Why don't you wait for a moment while I go get my coat."

Pete smiled and nodded.

"Oh, and do you mind driving?" Pete called after her, "For some reason—I don't know why—I seem to have left my car at home."

Beyond Here There Be Dragons

Notes

Part One

Chapter 1. Beyond Here There Be Dragons

The parable of the Chinese farmer and horse on page 11 is an adaptation of Taoist parable, accessed August 5, 2016, http://www.karmatube.org/videos.php?id=5625.

The quote from William Bridges on page 12 is from his book, *The Way of Transition: Embracing Life's Most Difficult Moments,* (2001) Perseus Publishing Cambridge, Massachusetts, p. 24.

The Rites of Passage by Arnold Van Gennep on page 13 is from his book, *The Rites of Passage,* translated by Vizedom, M. B. and Caffee, G. L., (1960) The University of Chicago Press, Chicago, p. 21. (Original work published 1909.) Van Gennep's book is considered a classic in the study of comparative religion and anthropology. Van Gennep saw rites as individual parts, pieces, or phases of a larger whole ritual movement. Other authors define "rite" and "ritual" differently. For purposes of simplification, I am using these two words interchangeably.

In contemporary America on page 13, minority religious and ethnic groups seem to do a better job at holding on to their rituals, perhaps in part out of a need to maintain their identity within the dominant culture. Notably, the Jewish traditions of sitting Shiva, saying kaddish, and the ritual for unveiling (dedicating) the grave marker, are good examples of rituals of transition. Another example is *Día de los Muertos* (Day of the Dead), an annual festive tradition in Mexico that is growing in popularity in the United States.

The quote from Ronald Grimes on page 13 is from his book, *Deeply into the Bone: Re-Inventing the Rites of Passages,* (2000) University of California Press, Berkeley, p. 254.

More information about the decline of the mourning period in the West is on page 14 Schillace, B., *Death's Summer Coat: What the History of Death and Dying Teaches Us about Life and Living, (2016)* Pegasus Books LLC, New York, pp. 124–125.

The value of an extended mourning period on page 14, is advocated by, Rosenblatt, P. C., Walsh, R. P., & Jackson, D. A., *Grief and Mourning in Cross-cultural Perspective,* (1976) HRAFS Press, New Haven, Connecticut. The authors suggest final death ceremonies, often weeks, months, or years later, may help mourners to take the necessary step to terminate mourning. "Moreover, a mourner who knows that a final ceremony is coming may do the psychological work necessary to accept the transition back to the state of being non-bereaved." p. 8.

Today grief educators on page 14-15, is articulated very clearly in Doka, K. J. and Tucci, A. S. editors, *Beyond Kübler-Ross: New Perspectives of Death, Dying and Grief, (2011)* Hospice Foundation of America, Washington, DC.

Chapter 2. Making Friends with Dragons

More about creation stories on page 17, can be found in, Sproul, B., *Primal Myths: Creation Myths Around the World*, (1997) Harper Collins, New York.

The Creation Story from the Hebrew scriptures on page 17, is from Genesis 1:6–8.

Leviathan citations from the Hebrew scriptures on page 17, can be found in Psalm 74:13–23, Psalm 104:26, Job 3:8, Job 41, and Isaiah 27:1.

Concerning the Dragons East and West discussion found on page 18, For a longer reflection on the dragon in cross-cultural comparison, see E. Ingersoll's, *Dragons and Dragon Lore,* (2014) Cosimo Classics, New York. Ingersoll's book, first published in 1928, compiles dragon mythologies from cultures across the globe. Despite different names and a diversity of form, he argues for a common origin in the preliterate humans' efforts to contend with the forces of nature in its many forms.

Move on page 19, People often say, "Don't make any major life decisions for at least a year." Generally, I think that is good advice. However, realistically, sometimes you have to sell the house or move for health or safety reasons. My advice: before you do something drastic, seek wise counsel. The problem is, once you do something like selling the house, you usually cannot get it back.

Music on page 20, the quote, as it was originally written, says savage "breast." Over time the *r* has often been dropped and the quote has been read as, "beast." However, I think it works well either way. Accessed September 15, 2016, http://www.goodreads.com/quotes/143494.

The quote from Rilke on page 21, is from his book, *Letters to a Young Poet,* Mitchell, S., Translated and foreword, (1984) First Vintage Books Edition, (1986) New York, p. 92.

Chapter 3. Dragons Thrive in Chaos

"Betwixt and between" by Victor Turner on page 24, is from his book, *The Forest of Symbols: Aspects of Nbembu Ritual,* (1967) Cornell University Press, New York.

Cultural Appropriation on page 24, Caution should be taken when designing your own rituals based on something you have heard or read about from another culture. The original meaning can get lost or distorted when used out of context. People who have been marginalized or oppressed consider the practice of *cultural appropriation*—borrowing rituals or other traditions from another culture without permission—as disrespectful and abusive.

Chapter 4. Wrestling with Dragons
The term "jury-rig," on page 32, as defined in Word Detective, was accessed December 26, 2016, http://www.worddetective.com/2012/01/jerry-rig-jury-rig/.

Chapter 5. The Dragon's Mark
Jacob on page 35, is from the Hebrew scriptures, Genesis 32:22–31.

Adulthood on page 37, It is possible that I am not being fair to van Gennep; he was quick to point out that physical puberty and social puberty are two distinct concepts. In chapter VI on Initiation Rites, he cites several examples, from different cultures, of multi-staged initiation rites that take place over an extended period of time, in some cases many years. My point is simply to illustrate the profound impact the death of the second parent can have on the psycho-social development of their adult children. van Gennep, A., *Rites of Passage*, pp. 65–115.

Sages from across the ages on page 37, In *The Ritual Process: Structure and Anti-Structure*, (1969), Transaction Publishers, Piscataway, NJ. Victor Turner suggests, "Prophets and artists tend to be liminal and marginal people, 'edgemen,' who strive with a passionate sincerity to rid themselves of the cliché … and to enter into vital relations with other men in fact or imagination." p.128. In addition to prophets and artists, I consider many of those whom my character Mico refers to as "sages from across the ages," as well as poets, professors, philosophers, counselors, and a fair number of clergy types to be, *edge-people.* They all see the world through different eyes. Primarily, their calling is to critique the prevailing wisdom (often at great personal cost). They have the ability to lift the veil for us and offer a momentary glimpse into the possibility of a better way.

Another quote by Rilke on pages 37-38, is from Rilke, R.M., *Letters to a Young Poet,* Mitchell, S., Translated and foreword, (1984) First Vintage Books Edition, (1986) New York, pp. 34–35.

Liminality as a state of reflection on page 38, The quote is from Turner, V., *The Forest of Symbols: Aspects of Ndembu Ritual,* (1967) Cornell University Press, New York, p. 105.

Chapter 6. Land Ho!
Helen Keller on page 43, The quote by **Keller** is from, *Let Us Have Faith,* (1940) Doubleday & Company, Garden City, New York. pp. 50, 51.

Chapter 7. The Heart of a Dragon
Medal for Courage on page 45, While there are few examples of rituals of reincorporation for the bereaved in our culture, perhaps there should be more! As with rituals of transition, the absence of culturally prescribed rituals marking the successful completion of a life transition means you can be creative and make up your own. In this case, I would strongly

recommend that you consider designing rituals with an audience in mind. Reincorporation presupposes a role for the community, if only one of having a witness or public affirmation of your self-proclaimed successful return. If the community will not offer a tangible token of remembrance, perhaps you might consider designing and investing yourself with your own medal of courage.

Chapter 8. The Last Horizon
Erik Erikson on page 49, Here, I am referring to Erikson's eighth stage of psychosocial development, "Integrity vs. Despair." In, *The Life Cycle Completed*, (1982) Norton, New York.
The quote by St. Teresa Benedicta of the Cross on page 50, A convert to Christianity, Edith Stein entered the convent and became a Carmelite nun, but because of her Jewish ancestry was sent to and died in the concentration camps during World War II. Accessed, February 5, 2017, http://carmelitesofboston.org/prayer/prayers-of-carmelite-saints/prayers-of-st-teresa-benedicta-of-the-cross-edith-stein/.
The End of the Journey on page 50, For more information read my article, *"Tears Flow Like a River,"* Re-joining the Sea, p. 4, accessed, February 5, 2017 http://www.griefriver.com.

Part Two

The Quote by Helen Keller on page 60, Keller, H., *The Open Door*, (1957) Doubleday, Garden City, New York.
The quote by St Teresa Benedicta of the Cross repeated on page 71, Ibid., Accessed, February 5, 2017, http://carmelitesofboston.org
Blessed are the eyes that have not seen and yet believe." on page 89, is from the Gospel of John, 20:29.

ABOUT THE AUTHOR

Thomas John Dennis, D. Min., LCPC, CT was born during the Chinese Year of the Dragon and gained his knowledge of these mythical beasts by wrestling with a few dragons of his own over the years. He is the creator of the *Grief River®* Model, a nature based framework for describing grief over the course of the lifespan. He is currently a hospice bereavement services coordinator in the Chicago area and maintains a private grief counseling practice in Galena, Illinois.

Visit *www.griefriver.com* for more information.

Made in the USA
Columbia, SC
19 May 2022